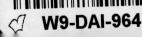

Studio Olafur Eliasson
The Kitchen

WITHDRAWN

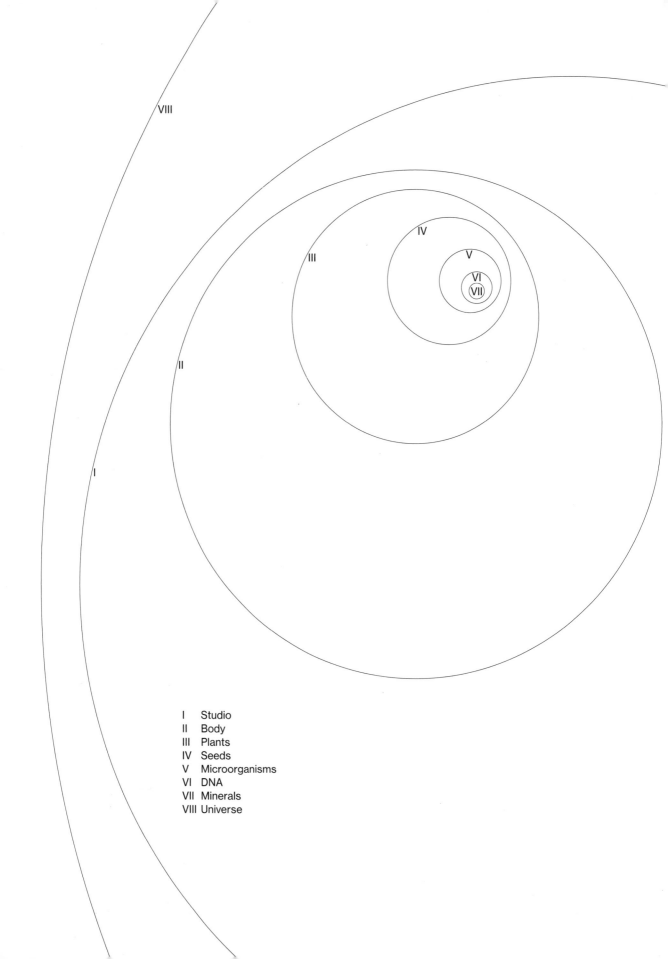

I   Studio
II   Body
III   Plants
IV   Seeds
V   Microorganisms
VI   DNA
VII Minerals
VIII Universe

Studio Olafur Eliasson
The Kitchen

Bacteria
enzyme — cheese
yeast — bread
(Frementation)

Johrgurt

soil

OUR
MAIN
PROTAN (Beans)
AND
SPICE
AND
OIL

OUR EVERYDAY
DISHES community
daily rutine

ietic thinking seed as food

aily rutine

Vegetables

Proteins, beans, grains, seeds

ATOM

DNA

?

Amino acid

Protein

GM soya

Radiation

HOW
WE
APPER
ON
EARTH

EARTH
&
MOON

big ban

SUN
SYSTEM

ells) / Eating / Digesting

Bacteria (micro organisms) / Soil / fermentation

Miner

A. Bodo   B. Cercobodo   C. Tetramitus   D. Naeglaria   E. Euglypha

F. Remoya   G. Balantiophorus   H. Colpoda   I. Uroleptus

The Kitchen is a collection of ideas and meals, and a portrait of Studio Olafur Eliasson. Throughout the week, studio members – including artists, architects, craftsmen, specialized technicians, art historians, and archivists – gather around the tables at lunchtime. Many dishes served at lunch have become favorites, among them recipes shared by studio members and friends. They appear in the book, ordered intuitively and yet always connected to the main focus of each chapter. Recurring subcategories are used to group certain stories and recipes associated with special events and encounters with visiting cooks and artists:

===========

Recipes

The sixty-person yield of the recipes reflects the ever-growing number of studio members for whom the kitchen team cooks. Not everyone will have the opportunity to cook for sixty eaters, so ingredients for six are also listed. Recipes for baking and preserving and for drinks are given in one base quantity and can easily be multiplied if needed.

===========

Events

Over the years, the studio has organized and hosted a wide range of events, whether alone, together with outside partners, or with the Institut für Raumexperimente (Institute for Spatial Experiments). Communal meals are often at the heart of these events, which are documented here with text, images, and recipes.

~~~~~~~~~~~

Encounters

Visitors to the studio will sometimes cook and eat around the kitchen table or engage in conversations about food, sharing, tasting, and sensing. These encounters are documented as an extension of the studio's kitchen table.

5

Contents

Every time I visit Berlin I make a point of going to see Olafur. I love being led through the rooms that make up his beautiful, rambling studio, housed in a converted brewery in Prenzlauer Berg, and hearing about the many projects he's taken on since our last reunion. Though getting a glimpse into Olafur's magical world is a rare pleasure – his study alone is a cabinet of wonders – I will confess that I usually try to time my visits to coincide with lunch. This is because lunch at Olafur's studio is no insignificant event – rather, it's an hour in which every one of his ninety employees comes together to sit at communal tables for a simple, nourishing and emphatically *delicious* family-style meal.

The last time I visited, in the middle of an icy February, Olafur was leaning across the table ladling bowls of steaming beet soup for guests and colleagues. Plates heaped with slices of freshly baked whole-grain bread spread with lemon zest butter and salad bowls full of leaves were being passed from person to person. Of course this meal, prepared by the wonderful kitchen team (led by Lauren Maurer and Asako Iwama, two chef-artists whom Olafur brought on some years ago), was delicious. But what somehow always strikes me most is how Olafur has managed to make this daily, civilized and convivial ritual such a central part of his studio's ecosystem. The kitchen, which he designed to sit more or less at the center of the large light-filled canteen, is in many ways

the heart of the whole place. That he decided to make this cookbook attests to the importance that Olafur places on the food that is made there – it sits alongside his art as one of the many strands of his multifaceted practice. And though the cooks, including Christine Bopp and, at times, Olafur's sister, Victoria Eliasdóttir, are largely responsible for the cooking that goes on, the rest of the staff are implicitly involved and take turns clearing the tables and washing the dishes once meals have drawn to a close.

In the way this kitchen and dining room organism works, I am reminded of two projects that are very close to my heart: the Rome Sustainable Food Project at the American Academy and the Edible Schoolyard Project in Berkeley, California. The Rome Sustainable Food Project came about almost by chance, when one of the trustees of the Academy asked me over dinner if I could do something about the lackluster food in the canteen there. I accepted but only very conditionally: everything had to be right, from planting an on-site garden, to sourcing local and biodynamic produce, to creating a kitchen internship program and making a commitment to composting and recycling. Somehow the Academy agreed and nearly ten years on, it is a thriving, central part of its identity.

There are many common threads between this project and what Olafur has undertaken in his studio, but perhaps the most obvious comparison is that both communities are made up of international crossdisciplinary artists, academics, and intellectuals. Before the project began at the Academy, resident fellows and researchers, as well as the Academy's staff, were

fleeing the campus in search of something decent to eat. The shift to providing something both delicious and wholesome brought people back to the table, literally. Conversations that never would have been – friendships between Classicists and painters, activists and furniture designers – were the products of the generosity of this culinary gesture. Olafur too, I think, saw the potential for these strands to develop, as if the table might become the site of new projects taking shape. Perhaps because his own practice depends on being able to move fluidly between media – from installation, to sculpture, to architecture, to video, to designing, marketing, and distributing his Little Sun solar lamp – he was able to see how food could become the bond between the people who make these diverse engagements possible. And not just a bond but a catalyst and an inspiration!

The other project I think of in light of Olafur's achievement is the Edible Schoolyard Project, which I started twenty years ago in Berkeley at Martin Luther King Jr. Middle School. It began as a garden to be farmed by students and a kitchen classroom where the products of their labor would, under the tutelage of a cooking teacher, become a shared meal. Today, those activities are woven into all aspects of the school's curriculum, from math to history and science, and our experiences there have helped us develop an edible education curriculum we hope eventually to implement in every school nationwide. Gardens and kitchens have the potential to be interactive classrooms, just as the table has the potential to be an incubator of ideas. Olafur's kitchen, in which the food is always simple and sustainable, could be a model

for school kitchens everywhere. He has demonstrated that the more beautiful and real the food – which itself is a kind of art – the richer the thought and the more fertile the dialogue.

Beauty is something that Olafur thinks about often – of course he does! – but beauty is also a way of communicating care. Just as employees might find more joy in work performed in a beautiful environment, children, I believe, are better able to learn if their surroundings reflect mindfulness. It was a commitment to beauty that in many ways served as the germ of inspiration for the original Edible Schoolyard in Berkeley (I saw the run-down school in my neighborhood and thought: *I must do something to make this place more beautiful!*) Of course, Olafur's book, like his studio, is a beautiful thing: full of gorgeous black-and-white photography, with plates of food and ingredients springing forward in colorful relief. We get a look, too, at his rooftop garden and the densely populated tables at lunchtime, alongside diagrams illustrating the variety of seeds, or the effects of planetary movements on the foods we eat and, through them, the amount of the sun's energy we ingest.

This is a wonderful book to sit with, page through, and be inspired by. But it is also a book that chronicles the very real culinary experiments that take place in Olafur's studio on a daily basis. These pages are full of approachable recipes to make delicious, local and seasonal food – whether for yourself, your family, a school or even a ninety-person studio. Olafur implores us to "take our time" and with this book, I feel, he is helping us all to do so, helping us to come back to our senses.

Studio Olafur Eliasson, Rungestrasse, Berlin, 1998–2002

Cooking is caring for others. It is a gesture of generosity and hospitality that functions as social glue; it amplifies social relations and translates thoughts into food, into giving and sharing. When we cook, we both use the world and produce it at the same time. And through eating, we take in the world, bringing light into our bodies. Take a piece of lettuce – it is essentially stored sunlight. Since the lettuce could not have grown without being exposed to the sun, you could say that it acts like a solar cell. By eating, we take in this energy.

The Kitchen celebrates the connections between human beings, food, and the sun as a system of energy exchange, as an ecology of giving and taking, of sharing. It examines food through various lenses, from the microscopic to the macroscopic.

I find it fascinating to do a book about something that everyone knows. Food is fundamental to human life. Eating is like breathing; we all do it to stay alive. To eat is to have an experience literally on the inside, and our knowledge of hunger and of food in our stomachs is, more than anything, a *felt knowledge.* Our experiences are embodied, ingrained in everyday life. This topic of embodiment has long been at the center of my artistic practice.

I like to think of my studio as a "reality-producing machine." Through the production of art, the studio has a direct effect on the city of Berlin, where it is located, and on the world beyond. It coproduces a slice of the times we live in, the values – political, ethical, and aesthetic – that influence our thoughts and actions.

The different parts of my studio are intertwined: the architects and designers develop installations and larger-scale built structures; the communications and publications team collects and disseminates information and ideas; the wood and metal workshops, painters, and skilled craftsmen test and produce, hands-on, the various artworks; and the office management and finance teams make sure the studio runs seamlessly, practically, and economically. One team influences the decisions of the others; one project feeds the next – the feeling of interdependence is key.

Feeding this entire interwoven organism is the kitchen. It quite literally supplies the energy that powers our daily activities.

The approximately ninety people working in the studio, across three floors, crowd into the kitchen each day at lunchtime. Sitting around one long table, sharing food, we take the opportunity to get inspiration from unexpected corners, while also engaging in pragmatic conversations about work, chitchat, or exchanging the odd piece of gossip. After lunch, rotating groups of studio members do the dishes and clean the tables. We treasure the sometimes unpredictable outcomes of our mealtimes.

The kitchen started out on a much smaller scale about thirteen years ago. At that time, studio members would take turns cooking for the rest of the team, then a group of about fifteen people. In 2005, when it became impractical to wait until four in the afternoon for the chicken to be served, it was

clear that someone was needed especially for the kitchen; that is when artist, food activist, and cook Asako Iwama was brought in to cook for the expanded team. She was joined six months later by Lauren Maurer, and for many years, the two ran the kitchen with great empathy and dedication, bringing with them specialized knowledge concerning the many issues surrounding cooking and food. The making of this book marked the conclusion of almost ten years of cooking and co-thinking by Asako, who has now gone on to pursue other projects. The kitchen team is now headed by Lauren Maurer, together with Christine Bopp,

Invalidenstrasse, Berlin, 2003–2008

Nora Wulff, and Montse Torredà Martí. The kitchen's approach, however, remains the same: the ingredients are organic; the dishes — with rare exceptions — are all vegetarian.

Over the years, the kitchen has also become a coproducer of many events: the studio-based *Life Is Space* symposia, where the shared meals and coffee breaks are as important as the diverse performances, experiments, and community thinking that take place there; the social gatherings that mark the openings of the irregular exhibitions at Grey Sheep, the studio project space housed next door; and, until recently, the various seminars and marathon workshops conceived by the team of the Institut für Raumexperimente, which often included food experiments, performances, drifts through Berlin, and a host of other activities. I set up the institute, in association with the Berlin University of the Arts, in 2009 as an experiment in arts education and hosted it one floor above my studio. Codirectors Christina Werner, Eric Ellingsen, and I cultivated experimentation and uncertainty for five years, working with the institute's twenty-five participants to turn thoughts into action.

Today we continue to invite friends and collaborators to eat with us, and, on a good day, some one hundred people may come together at the table in the kitchen to celebrate unexpected social encounters or to take a deep breath during the various doings of the day. Occasionally, people also come by to cook: among them, food activist Lynn Peemoeller; eminent cooks Alice Waters, Angelo Garro, René Redzepi, and Camilla Plum; artists Nico Dockx, Egon Hanfstingl, and Anne Duk Hee Jordan;

poet and thinker Pireeni Sundaralingam; and gallerist Zhang Wei. Icelandic cook Victoria Eliasdóttir, my sister, has also become a close ally of the kitchen team and works with them alongside running her own restaurant.

This book is a portrait of the studio kitchen. Yet it is also a portrait of the complex organism that is my studio from the perspective of the kitchen. Initially we wanted to make a publication just for the friends of the studio, to simply toss succulent recipes into a book the way you toss salad. But when you cook, you may end up with a slightly different meal from the one outlined in the recipe, and so this book

too has grown to incorporate the research, artistic projects, and food-thinking that take place in and around the studio kitchen. Since others may be as interested as we are in the interconnections between food, art-making, and daily life, we have now turned it into a book for a wider audience.

I hope it proves as much food for thought as it is satisfying to your hunger.

Pfefferberg, Berlin

The Body Is a Small Universe

Asako Iwama and
Lauren Maurer

Do I listen to my body's signals? Can I feel the vibration of my cells? How do I feel when I wake up in the morning? How are my organs? Touching and feeling my body, feeling the temperature of my skin, gently placing my hand to heal.

I might feel like eating clear, warm, salty soup or crunchy, toasted bread with honey and butter.

During the day, in the moment of doing, we find ourselves forgetting our body. There is a tightness in the neck and shoulders. We focus on breathing in and out.

We need to know how we feel in order to recognize the other.

The act of cooking is thinking and doing in fluid motion. Cooking is being in motion, navigating our sensations, connecting, and transforming. Resonating with each element in motion. It is an act of translation between kitchen and studio, my appetite and yours, different ingredients, tangible matter and idea, body and universe, wholeness and particle. It is the continuous transformation of nature and culture, serving and being served, expectation and satisfaction, akin to the moon tide, coming and leaving.

Cooking is being in the flow: the permeable skin between body, plants, seeds, microbes, minerals, sun, moon, planet Earth.

The continuous process of being enfolded into what we are and what we eat.

Being in the kitchen is to be present, to receive other life: plants grown and harvested become part of us when we eat. With full respect, we prepare the ingredients in a simple manner, keeping their flavor and texture. Intuition lets us listen and savor their taste. We prepare green beans, boiled quickly and sprinkled with salt. The kitchen is an alchemic space: fire and water, earth and air; the place where elements resonate. Being in a kitchen or garden, by thinking and learning, we transform ourselves.

The act of cooking is questioning.

Why do we need to eat? What do we want to eat? Where does the food come from? How did it grow? How do we eat – together or alone? What is the meaning of sharing? The meaning of hunger? These questions generate and navigate us. They form us. How will we commit?

Working together in our kitchen, we resonate with each other's rhythm. The awareness of being part of a larger whole roots us; practicalities help us to focus.

Cooking is a circular movement to meet the other.

Mind map created by Asako Iwama during the initial brainstorming process for *The Kitchen*

食料

low

tradition

culture

detachmen

sirious

enthusias

EATING

orlisum

taxonomy
分類

NARY
ion

classificat
organism
systemati

ive

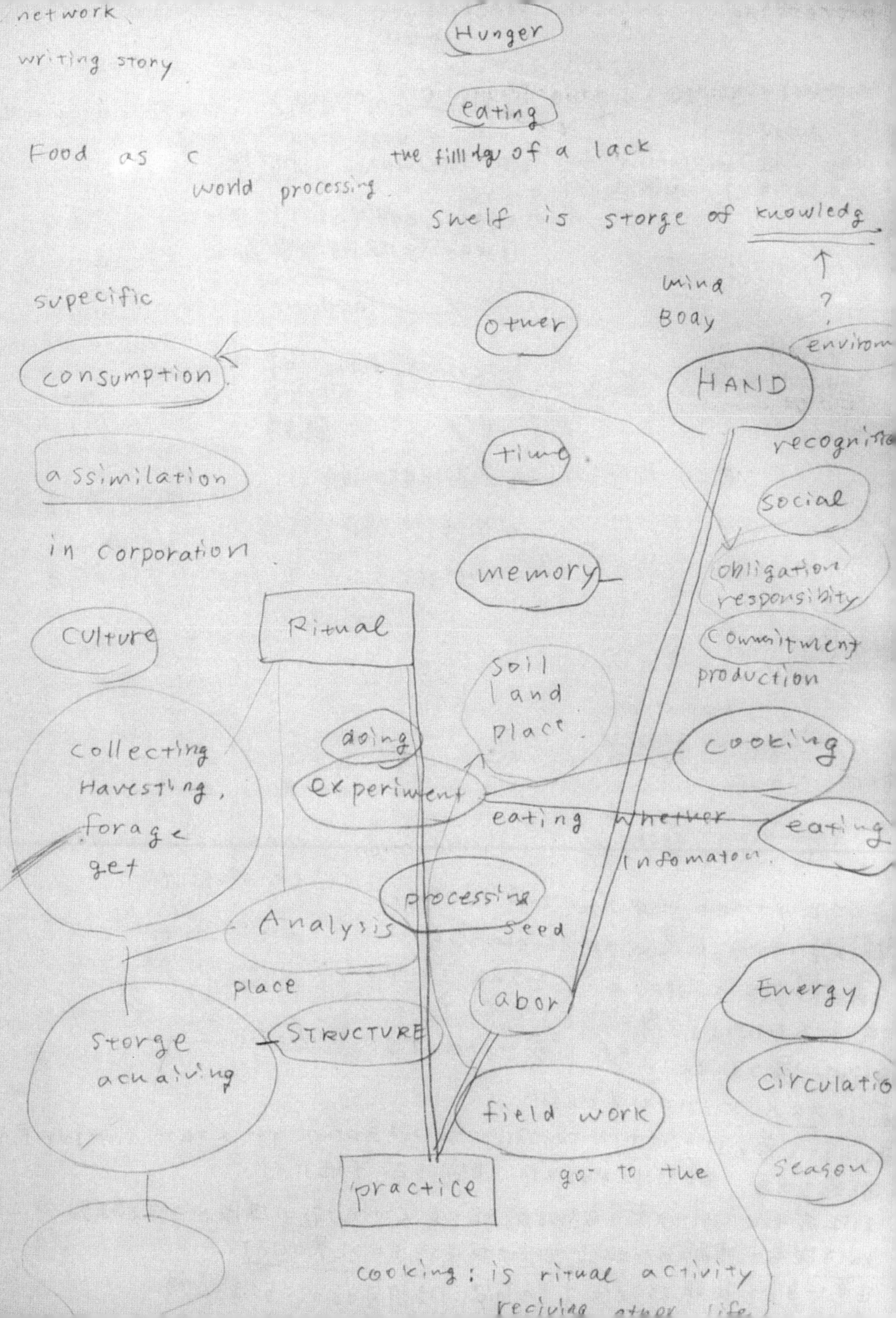

network

writing story.

Hunger

eating

Food as c   the fillidge of a lack

world processing

Shelf is storge of knowledg

supecific

Other

mind
Body

?

environm

consumption

HAND

recognize

assimilation

time

social

in corporation

memory

obligation
responsibity

Culture

Ritual

Soil
land
Place

Commitment
production

collecting
Havesting,
forage
get

doing

experiment

cooking

eating whether

eating

Infomaton.

Analysis

processing
seed

place

labor

Energy

Storge
achaiving

STRUCTURE

Circulatio

field work

Season

practice

go to the

cooking: is ritual activity
reciuing other life

Studio

Asako Iwama and
Lauren Maurer

When we started cooking for the studio team in 2005 – about fifteen people at the time – the studio was located on Invalidenstrasse, in an old railway storage space next to the Hamburger Bahnhof art museum. It was one big open space with the kitchen placed in the same room as the test area of the workshop and the architects, who worked in a "loft" above (and occasionally complained about sticky keyboards). It was cold in the winter and hot in the summer. The kitchen was a patchwork, a collage consisting of an antique wooden table, an old electric four-plate cooker, an unreliable oven, a dishwasher with a two-hour cycle, and two refrigerators that froze in the back. We hung a poster on the wall from Alice Waters's seminal cookbook *The Art of Simple Food* for everyone to see; it outlined her ideas on sharing and eating fresh, locally produced, organic food. In the mornings, honey, cheese, and bread were put out so that everybody could help him or herself to a small breakfast. The Icelandic geometer Einar Thorsteinn, the studio's longtime collaborator, brought his sourdough starter to the studio and baked unsalted bread with special Icelandic herbs on a regular basis.

We had a garden along the old railway tracks, where we had lunch and held meetings during summer or gathered for the Life Is Space seminars. Sometimes we had barbecues using a grill the workshop team had built from a barrel. Later, the team built a composter from another barrel. If we needed certain pans or pots customised for us, those in the workshop could do this too. Anything can be built at the studio.

In 2008, the studio, which had grown to about fifty people, moved to our current location, at Pfefferberg. We planned the new kitchen according to drawings by Asako, with help from the in-house architects, and it was built by the workshop team. In the new space, we have equipment to cook for more people, a research desk, a rooftop garden, and lots of new possibilities opened up here simply through our being in contact with the Grey Sheep project space and the Institut für Raumexperimente, with whom we collaborated on many occasions.

The studio is a place of communication and community. It is a platform for visions we share, but it is also a space that allows for friction. The kitchen is where we come together, with our different stories, to share nourishment. Lunchtime means encounters. Some guests come for meetings with Olafur, studio members, or the institute; some for seminars or workshops; some when they happen to pass through Berlin. Visitors spend time with us, enter into dialogue, join us, and inspire us in the translation process that is cooking. Sometimes we reach out and travel ourselves – to Antwerp, Belgium; Berkeley, California; Chicago, Illinois; or Beijing, China.

The kitchen team has grown and changed over the years, and many cooks have joined us for long or short spells, among them, Aykan Safoğlu, Thórdís Magnea Jónsdóttir, Julian Bethge, Anne Duk Hee Jordan, Derrick Wang, Montse Torredà Martí, and Christine Bopp. We come from different parts of the world, bringing with us different food concepts and traditions – from Japan, the United States, Germany, Spain, Turkey, and Iceland. These influences flow into the meals we plan and the way we prepare the food.

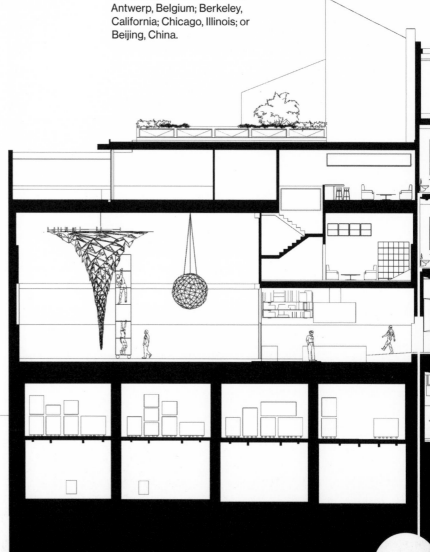

Our diverse interests are also reflected in our kitchen library: a collection of books on soil and composting, fermentation, macrobiotics, permaculture, biodynamic agriculture, seed banks, food politics, and a wide range of much-used and well-worn cookbooks. The quotes appearing throughout this book reflect some of our reading and represent the key thoughts that resonate with us and influence our cooking.

Our daily routine in the kitchen revolves around preparing lunch for the studio. Our food thinking is constantly evolving, and, over time, we have grown into a vegetarian kitchen, influenced by our interest in macrobiotics and biodynamic agriculture. Our work is to prepare seasonal ingredients carefully and thoughtfully into dishes that we hope meet people's hunger. We receive deliveries of organic produce every week, some of them directly from Apfeltraum, a biodynamic farm just outside Berlin, and some from BioInsel, a local organic shop. Every time

we set out to cook, diverse ingredients connect in a unique way: ultimately, we put our energy – and with it ourselves – into our cooking. The labor of human hands is part physical process, part imagination. This is why our recipes help navigate the act of cooking, but the process never produces the same dish. Our work is eaten by all. It becomes part of everybody gathered around the common table. Our eating together is an affirmation of life.

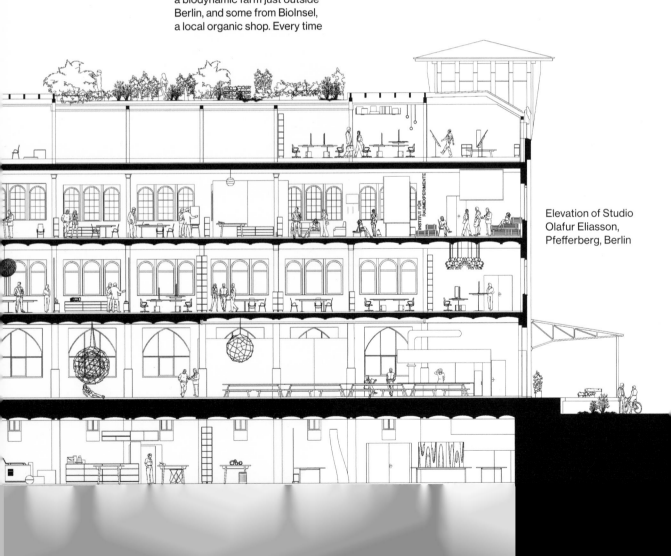

Elevation of Studio
Olafur Eliasson,
Pfefferberg, Berlin

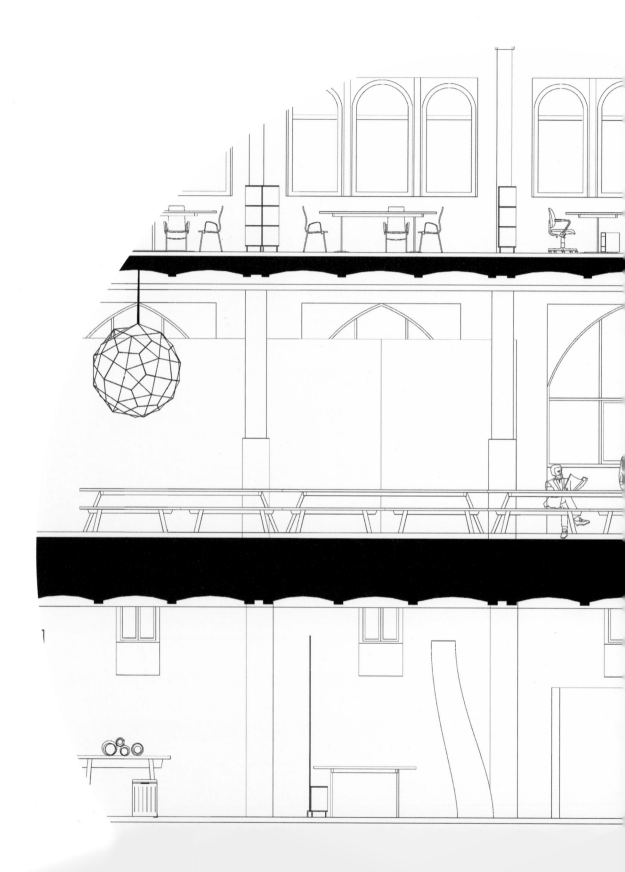

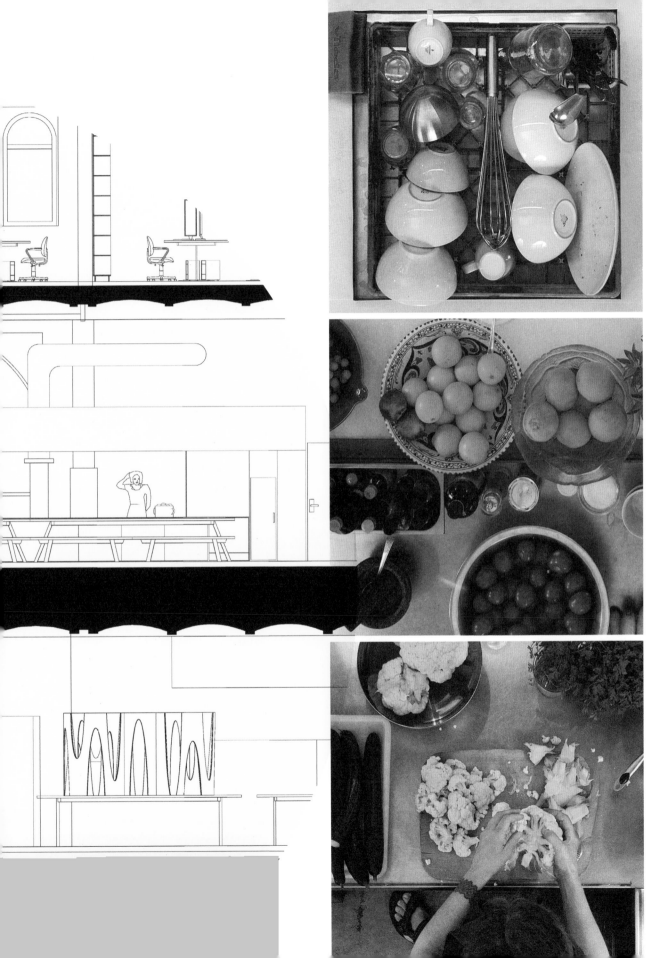

The studio team lines up
for lunch.

A sketch by Asako Iwama that
was used in planning the kitchen
of the Pfefferberg studio

"The very possibility of our being here, the very possibility of our living, is based on the lives of all kinds of beings that have gone before us – our parents, our mothers, the soil, the earthworm – and that is why the giving of food in Indian thought has been treated as the everyday *yagna,* or 'sacrifice,' that you have to perform. It is not the once-on-a-Sunday ritual, it is a ritual embodied in every meal, every day, all of the time, reflecting the recognition that giving is the condition of your very being. You do not give as an extra, you give because of your interdependence with all of life, your interdependence both with the human beings who make your life possible in your community, and with the non-human kith and family that we have."

‖ Vandana Shiva ‖
Annadāna: The Gift of Food

After lunch, studio members take turns washing the dishes and cleaning the kitchen.

Life Is Space (LIS) is a series of daylong events that have been organized by Studio Olafur Eliasson on four occasions since 2006. In a day of presentations, discussions, and experimentation, the studio team and participants from the Institut für Raumexperimente come together with friends and guests – scientists, artists, theorists, spatial practitioners, and movement experts. Each Life Is Space orbits, asteroid-like, around a general theme.

LIS 1 (June 2006) was inspired by the idea of "feelings as actions"; LIS 2 (June 2007) focused on the relation between models and reality; LIS 3 (May 2008) dealt with the relativity of light and color; and LIS 4 (June 2011) pursued ideas about embodied thought.

The informal structure of the events – with no distinction made between experiments, discussions, and casual conversations – results in a long suc-

cession of ideas, exercises, and an exploration of our senses. Conversations that take place during coffee and lunch breaks are as productive as presentations prepared in advance. To encourage such dialogue, food experiments have been integrated into the events since 2007. At LIS 2, for example, Danish chef René Redzepi served a series of dishes that dealt with our perception of time and space.

LIS 1, 2006

The food experiments of LIS concern the essential duality implicit in eating together: When I eat, it is an experience that is extremely individual. But by eating together with others, I situate my experience within a space that is very much collective – the meal, the act of eating together, the shared conversation. We convert into energy the same ingredients, prepared and seasoned in a similar way. It is therefore, in a sense, a common experience. But since you have a different set of taste buds, a different body, a different history, and different preferences, your experience may radically differ from mine. Of course, just as I can never be entirely certain that the color I call blue is the same blue for everyone else on the planet, taste is relative. What we have in common is that we are different.

Olafur Eliasson

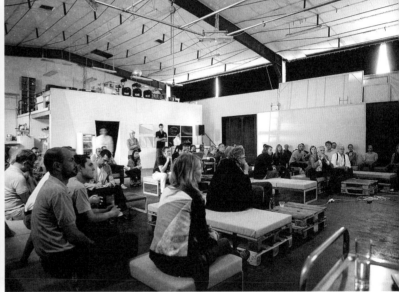

LIS 2, 2007: During the symposium, Danish chef René Redzepi presented a plateful of milk skin with grass, flowers, and herbs taken from the very field where the milk cow had grazed.

LIS 3, 2008. Corresponding to the theme of the symposium, Asako Iwama and Lauren Maurer explored how colors enter our body through food.

LIS 4, 2011. For this event, Danish chef Camilla Plum took over the metal workshop to prepare a delicious summer barbecue with shrimp salad.

Day-Before-Life-Is-Space Marathon, 2011. For LIS 4, Lynn Peemoeller, Fotini Lazaridou-Hatzigoga, and the Institute für Raumexperimente created a taste experiment that isolated five different flavor groups and encouraged participants to draw a diagram translating the taste into a shape.

Three-Cheese Quiche   Serves 6–8

1	Tart and Pie Dough (see below)
	flour, for dusting
½ cup (100 g)	mozzarella, cubed
3	eggs
1⅔ cups (400 ml)	crème fraîche
½ cup (100 g)	parmesan, grated
½ cup (100 g)	gruyère, grated
	salt and freshly ground black pepper

Preheat the oven to 350°F/180°C/Gas Mark 4.

Roll out the dough on a lightly floured surface, from the center out, forming a circle slightly bigger than your pie dish. Drape the dough over the rolling pin and move it into the dish. Press gently against the sides of the form and fold over the edges, making sure that it stays a bit higher than the rim to prevent it from sinking in the heat of the oven. Poke the rolled-out dough in several places with a fork and refrigerate for 30 minutes. Place a piece of parchment (baking) paper slightly bigger than the size of the dish onto the dough and add beans or pastry weights. Bake for 10 minutes and cool slightly.

Spread the mozzarella over the prebaked crust. Mix together the eggs, crème fraîche, parmesan, and gruyère and season with salt and pepper. Pour the egg mixture evenly over the mozzarella and bake in the middle of the oven for 30 minutes. If the top begins to turn too brown, cover with aluminum foil and bake further. Let the quiche cool for a few minutes before removing from the dish or cutting.

Variations
Also very nice with pear, gorgonzola, and leek; caramelized onions and feta with thyme and rosemary; or cooked fennel with tarragon. Prepare the egg mixture as described above and mix with a combination of your choice. Fill crust and bake.

Tart and Pie Dough   Makes one 9-inch (26 cm) piecrust

¾ cup (180 g)	cold butter, cubed
1 cup (250 g)	all-purpose flour
½ tsp	salt (omit if using salted butter)

Adapted from *The Art of Simple Food*

In a bowl, work the butter into the flour with your fingertips until the mixture resembles bread crumbs. This should be done as quickly as possible. Pour in ½ cup (125 ml) ice-cold water while stirring with a fork until it becomes dough. Form into a ball and let rest, refrigerated, for 30 minutes.

Baked Beets with Horseradish Dill Almond Sauce   Serves 6 | 60

Adapted from *Moro East*

1 medium | 11 lb (5 kg)	beets (beetroot), unpeeled
1¾ oz (50 g) | 1 lb 2 oz (500 g) . .	whole almonds, blanched
1½ oz (40 g) | 14 oz (400 g) . . .	finely grated horseradish
1 | 10 TB	sherry vinegar
. . . .	salt and freshly ground black pepper
3½ oz (100 ml) | 1¾ pints (1 liter) .	heavy (double) cream
1 | 10 TB	milk or almond milk
1 tsp | 1 bunch	dill, finely chopped

Preheat the oven to 425°F/ 220°C/Gas Mark 7.

Place the unpeeled beets on a baking sheet (tray), cover with aluminum foil, and bake for 50 minutes or until tender. Let cool until ready to handle, then peel and slice.

About 30 minutes before the beets are ready, prepare the sauce. Place the almonds in a food processor and pulse until fine, leaving a few small chunks for texture. Transfer to a mixing bowl and add the horseradish. Stir in the vinegar and season with salt and pepper. Just before serving, stir in the cream, milk, and dill. Do not overmix or the sauce will become solid. Check and adjust seasonings. Serve the beets hot or cold with the sauce.

We made scones more often at the Invalidenstrasse studio, when we were fewer people – usually Savory Scones to accompany soups like the Creamy Pink Root Soup with Roasted Kohlrabi (see page 162). The delicious Maple Syrup Scones are perfect for brunch. These days, when we bake for the whole studio, we multiply the recipes by six to make about one hundred.

Savory Scones   Makes about 15 scones

3¾ cups (450 g)	all-purpose flour, plus extra for dusting
4 tsp	baking powder (sodium bicarbonate)
1 tsp	salt
1 tsp	mustard
⅔ cup (150 ml)	milk
⅔ cup (150 g)	cold butter, cubed
7 oz (200 g)	parmesan or other strong hard cheese, finely grated, or feta, crumbled
4 TB	fresh herbs or scallions (spring onions), chopped
1	egg

Preheat the oven to 400°F/200°C/Gas Mark 6.

In a large bowl, mix the flour, baking powder, and salt. In another bowl, mix the mustard into the milk. Add the butter to the flour and massage it lightly with your fingers until the mixture resembles bread crumbs. Add the cheese and the herbs or scallions and mix. Carefully pour the milk into the flour mixture, stirring together first with a fork and then by hand to make a soft but firm dough, being sure not to overwork it.

Dust a work surface with flour and roll out the dough into a circle about 1 inch (2 cm) thick. Using a knife, cut the circle into quarters and then into quarters again, to make eight triangles. Alternatively, a round biscuit cutter can be used.

Place the dough on a lined baking sheet (tray). Beat the egg and brush on the scones with a pastry brush. Bake for 20 minutes until golden brown. Best eaten warm!

Maple Syrup Scones   Makes 12 scones

Adapted from *Breakfast, Lunch, Tea: Rose Bakery*

2 cups (250 g)	all-purpose flour, plus extra for dusting
⅔ cup (100 g)	whole wheat (wholemeal) flour
¼ cup (25 g)	rolled oats
1 TB	baking powder (sodium bicarbonate)
1 TB	caster sugar
½ tsp	salt
4 TB	maple syrup
4 TB	buttermilk
12 TB (160 g)	cold unsalted butter, cubed
1	egg

Preheat the oven to 400°F/200°C/Gas Mark 6.

In a large bowl, mix the flours with the oats, baking powder, sugar, and salt. In another bowl, mix together the syrup and buttermilk. Add the butter to the flour mixture and massage it lightly with your fingertips until the mixture resembles bread crumbs. Carefully pour the milk mixture into the flour mixture, stirring together first with a fork and then by hand to make a soft but firm dough, being sure not to overwork it.

Dust a work surface with flour and roll out the dough into a circle about 1 inch (2 cm) thick. Using a knife, cut the circle into quarters and then into quarters again, to make eight triangles. Alternatively, a round biscuit cutter can be used.

Place the dough on a lined baking sheet (tray). Beat the egg and brush on the scones with a pastry brush. Bake for 20 minutes until golden brown. Like the savory ones, these scones are best when eaten warm!

When René Redzepi came to visit the studio to contribute food experiments to the Life is Space 2007 seminar, he and his team expanded the planned menu spontaneously to include dandelion leaves and wood sorrel they had foraged in the studio garden. René's recipe with wood sorrel and sheep's milk here reminds us of the famed milk skin with grass he cooked for us at the seminar.

Rhubarb and Sheep's Milk with Wood Sorrel   Serves 4

By René Redzepi

Rhubarb Compote

1 lb 2 oz (500 g)	fresh rhubarb juice
1½ oz (40 g)	aronia juice
7 oz (200 g)	rhubarb stalks
1¾ oz (50 g)	birch syrup

Sheep's Milk

1 lb 2 oz (500 g)	cream
10½ oz (300 g)	egg whites
3½ oz (100 g)	sugar
8 sheets	gelatin
1 lb 5 oz (600 g)	sheep's milk yogurt

Rose Root Oil

10½ oz (300 g)	grapeseed oil
3½ oz (100 g)	rose root

To Serve

. . . .	Rhubarb Compote
. . . .	Sheep's Milk
. . . .	salt
. . . .	raw liquorice powder (dark)
4 handfuls	wood sorrel leaves
. . . .	Rose Root Oil
¼ oz (5 g)	fresh rhubarb juice, for serving

Special equipment . . . . a dehydrator
. . . . a sous-vide bag

Make the Rhubarb Compote
Ahead of time, and separately, reduce the rhubarb and aronia juices in a dehydrator until thick and syrupy. To make the rhubarb reduction, measure out 3½ oz (100 g) of the reduced rhubarb juice and combine it with ¾ oz (20 g) of birch syrup. Set aside reduced rhubarb and aronia juices and the rhubarb reduction until needed.

Using only the red parts of the rhubarb stems, place them into a sous-vide bag with the remaining 1 oz (30 g) birch syrup and 4 g of the reduced aronia juice and steam for 18 minutes at 158°F/70°C. Cut the cooked rhubarb into 2¾-inch (7 cm) thin strips, place in a 4-quart (1 liter) container with the cooking liquid and dry in a dehydrator. Baste and flip the strips in the cooking liquid every 45 minutes for the first 3 hours. For the next 2 hours, baste and flip every 20 minutes, adding rhubarb reduction as necessary. Cut rhubarb into ½-inch (1 cm) pieces and season with rhubarb reduction and fresh rhubarb juice.

Make the Sheep's Milk
Whip cream into soft peaks. Whip egg whites and sugar into a soft meringue. Bloom and then melt the gelatin in half the yogurt and when cooled add the rest of the yogurt. Lastly, fold in the whipped cream and egg whites. Set aside 10½ oz (300 g) in a 2 cup (500 ml) container.

Make the Rose Root Oil
Combine grapeseed oil with rose root and set aside.

To Serve
Place a scoop of rhubarb compote on each plate, next to it, scoop out a spoonful of the sheep's milk (like fresh cheese) and season with salt and liquorice powder. Build wood sorrel on top. Pour a generous spoon of the rose root oil on the side of the rhubarb along with some fresh rhubarb juice.

Awakening Our Senses   Alice Waters

Olafur and I met in Davos, Switzerland, one winter, where we were both unlikely participants at the World Economic Forum. We realized immediately that we were in the same business: the business of awakening people's senses. As my daughter, Fanny, wrote, Olafur's art "is like sitting down to a meal, a necessary human function, but one of tremendous sensuous possibility that makes you feel viscerally connected to something outside yourself."

So it came as no surprise, when I was invited to his Berlin studio not long after, to see how the feeding of his many collaborators forms an integral part of his artistic enterprise. After all, the most literal visceral connection we make is with food. Nor was it a surprise to learn that we share an unshakable commitment to local sustainable sources for the food we serve.

It was a rare privilege to cook a meal in the cathedral-like kitchen of Olafur's studio and serve it on that long, solid table. And after his cooks, Asako and Lauren, had come and worked with us in California, we collaborated again on an unforgettable dinner at the Museum of Contemporary Art in Chicago, in conjunction with Olafur's show there. I tried to create a meal that could complement Olafur's work both in the way it slowed down time and how it concentrated the senses.

The acts of art-making and cooking align in many ways; both reactive and creative, they mimic and accommodate each other. Good food makes the dining table into a place apart, a place where our animal need to feed can be exquisitely met, and space is cleared for our human dreams and desires. The kitchen at Olafur's studio replicates what happens around tables at my restaurant Chez Panisse and in the homes of cooks and artists every day: affordable, seasonal food is mindfully prepared and eaten together with family and friends, providing a respite out of which fresh ideas flourish. Too often, eating well is sacrificed in a misguided attempt to streamline our lives. Olafur's ability to recognize the folly of this sacrifice is, for me, one of the most attractive parts of his genius.

When Alice Waters came to visit us in the studio in February 2010, she and her friend Angelo Garro made fresh Focaccia with Salsa Verde (see page 58) and pulled pork.

Preparing food for the opening of the exhibition *Take your time: Olafur Eliasson* in Chicago, April 2009. Alice Waters flew in to cook for the opening.

Top right: Bob Cannard's Garden, Petaluma, CA, a sustainable farm that provides produce to Alice Waters's restaurant Chez Panisse.

Bottom right: One of Alice Waters' Edible Schoolyard Gardens, part of a program for edible education that teaches students about organic gardening and nutrition. This particular garden is in Berkeley, CA.

Bob Cannard's Garden,
Petaluma, CA

Alice Waters' Edible Schoolyard
Garden, Berkeley, CA

Focaccia   Makes 1 large or 6 small focaccia/s

By Alice Waters

2 tsp. . . . . dry yeast
3¼ cups (400 g) . . . . . . all-purpose flour, plus extra for dusting
1 tsp . . . . Maldon sea salt, plus extra to taste
. . . . freshly ground black pepper
2 TB . . . . extra virgin olive oil, plus extra for drizzling
. . . . fresh herbs, chopped

Mix the yeast with 1 cup (225 ml) warm water in a bowl and let sit for about 5 minutes. Put the flour and 1 teaspoon salt into the food processor. Add the dissolved yeast and 2 tablespoons olive oil. Pulse until a dough forms. If necessary, add more flour. The dough should be smooth but not sticky. Grease a large bowl with olive oil. Transfer the dough from the processor to a clean, lightly floured surface and knead it for a few minutes with your hands. Shape into a ball and place in the greased bowl. Cover with a cloth and leave to rise in a warm place for about 45 minutes.

Uncover and punch the dough a couple of times with your fists to deflate it. Working in the bowl, knead the dough four or five times. Cover and allow to rise again in a warm place for an additional 30 minutes.

Preheat the oven to 425°F/ 225°C/Gas Mark 7. Roll out the dough to a thickness of ½ inch (1 cm)and place on a baking sheet (tray). Alternatively, form six small rounds and place on your tray. Poke small indentations into the dough with your finger. Lightly brush or drizzle the dough with olive oil and sprinkle with salt, pepper, and herbs. Bake for 10 minutes, or until lightly golden. The small focaccias will be done faster.

Salsa Verde   Makes about 1 cup (200 ml)

By Alice Waters

2 bunches . . . . flat-leaf parsley, coarsely chopped
1 . . . . lemon, zested
1 small clove . . . . . . garlic, crushed or finely chopped
1 TB . . . . capers, coarsely chopped
½ cup (125 ml) . . . . . . olive oil
. . . . salt

Mix all ingredients well, taste and add salt if needed. Let the salsa sit for a while to develop the flavors.

Note
You can also add a little chopped salt-packed anchovy fillet, chopped shallot, or chopped hard-boiled egg – or all three. Lemon juice or vinegar makes the sauce zestier, but add them just before serving, as the acid will cause the herbs to discolor. If adding the chopped shallot, you can also let it macerate first in the vinegar or lemon.

Green Salad with
Balsamic Dijon Dressing
see page 353

Béchamel and Tomato Sauce
see page 62

Lasagna with Eggplant and Chard   Serves 6–8

about 2 lb (800 g)	Fresh Pasta (see below) or dry lasagna
2 cups (500 ml)	Tomato Sauce (see page 62)
2 cups (500 ml)	Béchamel Sauce (see page 62)
about 1 lb 5 oz (600 g)	eggplant (aubergine)
	salt and freshly ground black pepper
2 TB	olive oil, plus extra for the eggplant
1 large bunch	green or rainbow chard, stemmed
2 TB	butter
1	onion, finely chopped
3 cloves	garlic, finely chopped
scant ½ cup (100 ml)	dry white wine
5 oz (150 g)	mozzarella, thinly sliced (or goat cheese or extra béchamel)
⅔ cup (150 g)	grated parmesan or pecorino romano

Prepare the Fresh Pasta, Tomato Sauce, and Béchamel Sauce. If using fresh pasta dough, roll it out and set on towels to dry while you prepare the vegetables. Boil until it just starts to soften. You can also do this with dry pasta, though this is not necessary if an adequate amount of sauce is used. Cut the eggplant lengthwise into ½-inch (1 cm) slices, sprinkle with salt, and set aside for 30 minutes.

Preheat the oven to 400°F/ 200°C/Gas Mark 6.

Rinse the eggplant and pat dry, with paper towels. Brush with olive oil and bake, turning once, for about 20 minutes until browned. Chop the stems and the leaves of the chard but keep them separated. Heat the oil and butter in a large skillet, and cook the onion and garlic over medium heat for

3 minutes. Add the chard stems, sprinkle with salt and cook for about 5 minutes. Add the wine and the chard leaves; cover and cook until the chard is tender, for about 3 minutes. Season to taste with salt and pepper.

Oil the baking dish. Spread a layer of tomato sauce over the bottom of the dish and cover with a layer of pasta. Top with a quarter of the eggplant, then a quarter of the chard. Sprinkle with mozzarella and parmesan, and add a layer of tomato sauce and a layer of of béchamel. Cover with a layer of pasta and continue for 3 more layers, ending with pasta, sauces, and cheese if using fresh pasta, and ending with vegetables, sauces, and cheese if using dried pasta. Bake for 20 to 30 minutes, or until heated through.

Fresh Pasta   Makes 2½ lb (1 kg)

Scant 6 cups (700 g)	pasta flour or all-purpose flour
⅔ cup (100 g)	semolina flour
½ tsp	sea salt
4	whole eggs
9	egg yolks

Put the flours and salt in a food processor and add the eggs and egg yolks. Pulse-blend until the pasta begins to come together into a loose ball of dough. Knead the pasta dough until it is very stiff. You may have to blend in another whole egg. Cut the dough into eight equal-size pieces and briefly knead them into individual balls. Wrap each ball in plastic wrap and place in the refrigerator for at least 20 minutes (but for no longer than 2 hours).

Roll the dough through a pasta machine at the thickest setting 10 times. After each time through the machine, fold the sheet of dough in thirds to get a short, thick strip and run it through the machine again. After 10 such rolls with the machine, the pasta will begin to feel silky. At this point, you can set the machine to the specific thinness required: for tagliatelle, 1.5 mm; for ravioli, 0.5 mm.

If rolling by hand, you will have to hand-knead and hand-roll the dough the equivalent of 10 times through the machine. This needs to be done in a cool place so that the pasta does not dry out.

Tomato Sauce   Makes about 2¼ cups (500 ml)

6 TB	olive oil
1 medium	onion, minced
2 cloves	garlic, minced
2 small	red chiles, crushed
1 stalk	celery, minced
2	carrots, minced
2 cans (14 oz/400 g each)	tomatoes
2 tsp each	thyme and rosemary
2	bay leaves
	salt and freshly ground black pepper

Heat the olive oil in a heavy-bottom saucepan and gently cook the onions over medium heat until golden. Add the garlic and chiles and continue to cook for 2 minutes. Stir in the celery and carrots and cook until they begin to soften, stirring occasionally.

Add the tomatoes, thyme, rosemary, bay leaves, salt, and pepper and bring to a gentle simmer. Lower the heat and let simmer for about 20 minutes until the sauce thickens and reduces. Discard the bay leaves before serving.

With fresh tomatoes

2¼ lb (1.5 kg)	ripe tomatoes
2 TB	olive oil or butter, plus extra
3 TB	fresh basil, chopped (or 2 TB marjoram, chopped)
2 cloves	garlic, finely minced
	salt and freshly ground black pepper

Bring a pot of water to a boil and add the tomatoes for 2 minutes, until the skins loosen. Remove the tomatoes from the water and, when cool to the touch, peel and coarsely chop. Heat the oil or butter in a heavy-bottom saucepan and gently fry the garlic over medium heat for 1–2 minutes. Lower the heat and add the tomatoes and basil or marjoram. Simmer gently for 10 minutes until the tomatoes begin to break down. Add salt and pepper and another splash of olive oil.

Béchamel Sauce   Makes about 2¼ cups (500 ml)

3 TB	butter or vegetable oil
3 TB	all-purpose flour
2¼ cups (500 ml)	milk, warmed
	salt and white pepper
	a pinch of nutmeg

Melt the butter in a heavy-bottom pot and whisk in the flour a bit at a time. Cook over medium heat for 3 minutes, stirring constantly. Slowly add the milk, stirring constantly, to avoid lumps. Bring to a boil, continuing to stir, then reduce the heat to low and simmer for about 10 minutes, stirring often. The consistency should be a bit like yogurt. Add the salt, pepper, and nutmeg. Serve immediately or keep warm.

(Our lasagna is made with this béchamel. It's also delicious as a gratin with baked chicory or in macaroni and cheese.)

Making Dim Sum Dumplings (see page 69) in the studio, 2012

Making Baozi (see page 66) at The Pavilion, Beijing, 2012

Making Baozi (see page 66) with Zhang Wei in the studio, 2012

Dumplings

When Asako visited Beijing in the summer of 2012, a friend took her to The Pavilion, an independent art space run by Zhang Wei and artist and poet Hu Fang. Wei had brought some flour from a trip to Qingdao, in northeast China, which was sitting in small cotton bags on the windowsill. The flour had come from an organic farm where crops are grown in accordance with the traditional Chinese lunar calendar. Wei, Fang, and Asako were to make dumplings for dinner. A few days earlier, a handful of studio members had joined in the kitchen to make vegetarian Dim Sum Dumplings in Berlin. In 2013, Wei visited the studio and made large yeasted dumplings, called baozi.

Baozi   Makes about 12 large dumplings

By Zhang Wei

For the dough

6 oz (16 g)	fresh yeast
1⅔ cups (200 g)	all-purpose flour, plus extra for dusting
. . . .	sunflower oil, for greasing

For the filling

4	zucchini, coarsely grated
. . . .	salt
4	eggs
4	scallions (spring onions), finely chopped
3½ oz (100 g)	dry glass noodles, cooked and coarsely chopped
½ TB	sunflower oil
1½ TB	soy sauce
1 tsp	sugar

For the sauce

1 thumb-size piece	ginger, grated
½ TB	soy sauce
2 TB	rice vinegar
1 pinch	sugar
Also needed	bamboo steamer baskets with lids, matching large pot, cheesecloth. A metal steamer can also be used.

Crumble the fresh yeast and mix with ¼ cup (40 ml) warm water in a bowl. Let sit for about 5 minutes. Put the flour into the food processor. Add the dissolved yeast. Pulse until a dough forms. If necessary, add more flour. The dough should be smooth but not sticky. Grease a large bowl with sunflower oil. Transfer the dough from the processor to a clean, lightly floured surface and knead it for a few minutes with your hands. Shape into a ball and place into the greased bowl. Cover with a cloth and leave to rise in a warm place for about 45 minutes.

While waiting for the dough to rise, prepare the filling. Place the grated zucchini in a bowl and lightly sprinkle with a pinch of salt. Let stand. Scramble and cook the eggs. Taking a handful at a time, gently squeeze the soaked zucchini over the sink. It should lose excess moisture but not be squeezed dry. Mix with the scallions, glass noodles, and the scrambled eggs in a large bowl and add the sunflower oil, soy sauce, sugar, and salt to taste. Cover the dish. Uncover the risen dough and punch a couple of times with your fist to deflate it. Working in the bowl, knead the dough 4 or 5 times. Cover and let rise again in a warm place for an additional 30 minutes. Uncover, punch again, and knead another 4 or 5 times in the bowl.

For the sauce, mix the ginger, soy sauce, a small splash of rice vinegar, and a little sugar. Pour into small dishes, one per person, and set aside.

Lightly flour a clean surface. Pull off sections of dough the size of a small mandarin, form into rough balls.

Roll out the balls into flat rounds of about 4 inches (10 cm), turning them as you go. Make sure the edges are thinner than the center, which will hold the filling.

Place 2 teaspoons of filling in the center of each round. Gently form the baozi by pulling up the edges, and closing them in the middle by twisting.

Fill a pot with water, cover with a lid, and bring to a boil. Place a wet cheesecloth inside the bamboo steamer, overlapping its sides.

Place the baozi inside, making sure they don't touch. Place a lid on the steamer, leaving the cheesecloth edges hanging out. Uncover the pot, check that the water is still boiling, and place the steamer basket on top. The first round may take 12 to 15 minutes to cook; the next ones might be faster.

Lift the baozi gently from the steamer basket and place on a platter. Eat them by hand, dipping them into the sauce. They are also delicious eaten cold.

Variations
All kinds of vegetable- or meat-based options can be used. A sweet variation: Fill the baozi with Azuki Bean Paste (see page 318), add sugar and roasted sesame seeds, and serve for dessert with a cup of jasmine tea.

Dim Sum Dumplings   Makes about 30 small dumplings

1⅔ cups (200 g) . . . . all-purpose flour
. . . . Baozi filling (see page 66)
. . . . Baozi sauce (see page 66)

Also needed . . . . bamboo steamer baskets with lids, matching large pot. A metal steamer can also be used.

Place the flour in a bowl and add 7 tablespoons (100 ml) water gradually, in two or three rounds. Mix until a ball forms and all the flour is worked in. Set aside for 30 minutes, covering the bowl with a moist tea towel. Prepare the Baozi filling and the sauce, and set aside.

Put the dough on a clean work surface and knead it until silky. Form a long roll of dough and cut it into 1 inch (2 to 3 cm) long sections. Roll into balls, and then press them into disks.

Place a small teaspoon of filling into the center of each disk.

Wet the outer edges, fold in half, wet the edges again, then pinch and fold.

Fill a pot with water, cover with a lid, and bring to a boil. Place the dumplings inside the bamboo steamer. Place a lid on the steamer, uncover the pot, check that the water is still boiling, and place the steamer basket on top. The first round may take 10 to 12 minutes to cook; the next ones might be faster.

Variations
For fried dumplings, heat a pan until very hot and add sunflower oil. Set the dumplings inside, cover, and fry for 2 minutes over medium heat. Mix 1 tablespoon flour with 7 tablespoons (100 ml) water and add to the dumplings, covering the pan once more. Let cook until all the water has evaporated, about 10 minutes. Serve with sauce for dipping.

Pasta e Ceci   Serves 6 | 60

4 TB	2½ cups (600 ml)	olive oil or butter, plus more for serving
2 medium	9 lb (4 kg)	onions, diced
2 stalks	2 heads	celery, stalks and leaves, chopped
1 clove	1 head	garlic, minced
2 TB	4 bunches	rosemary, finely chopped
3	30	small red spicy dried chiles, crushed
. . . .	salt and freshly ground black pepper
3	30 cans (14 oz/400 g each) .	diced tomatoes
2	10	bay leaves
6¼ cups (1.5 liters)	3½ gallons (14 liters)	vegetable stock (broth) or water (liquid from cooked chickpeas can also be used)
1	18 can/s (14 oz/400 g each) .	chickpeas (or 4½ oz (135 g)	4½ lb (2 kg) dried chickpeas, soaked overnight and cooked)
1½ lb (600 g)	13 lbs (6 kg) . . .	volanti pasta
1 TB	4 bunches	flat-leaf parsley, chopped
. . . .	grated parmesan
. . . .	parmesan, for serving

Heat the olive oil or butter in a heavy-bottom saucepan, and gently fry the onions and celery over medium heat until lightly browned. Add the garlic, rosemary, chiles, and a pinch of salt and continue to cook, stirring for several minutes to combine the flavors. Add the tomatoes and bay leaves and cook for 15 minutes, stirring often. Add the broth or water and the chickpeas and cook for an additional 20 minutes. Add the pasta and simmer until al dente. Season with salt and pepper. Remove the bay leaves. Drizzle with olive oil and sprinkle with parsley and parmesan to serve.

Pressed Salad with Lemon and Ume   Serves 6 | 60

1	10	daikon (white radish), sliced in thin rounds
1 tsp	3 TB	sea salt
½	5	lemon/s, juiced
2 tsp	6 TB	ume su (see page 241)
1 tsp	4 TB	ume paste
1 stem	2 bunches	dill, finely chopped

Sprinkle the daikon with salt and mix by hand. Set in a bowl, cover with a plate and a heavy weight, and set aside for 15 minutes. Squeeze the radish to remove excess liquid. Stir in the lemon juice, ume su, ume paste, and the dill and mix well.

Note
Variations of this salad can be made with finely sliced cucumber, Chinese cabbage, celery, fennel, or carrots. Vary the dressing with ginger, sesame, and coriander or parsley.

Penne with Ginger and Tomato   Serves 6 | 60

By Derrick Wang, former member of the kitchen team
Adapted from *River Café Cookbook Green*

4 cloves | 3 head	garlic, chopped
⅔ cup (150 ml) |	
6¼ cups (1.5 liters)	olive oil
5 oz (150 g) | 3¼ lb (1.5 kg) . . .	ginger, finely chopped
3 small | a handful	dried red chiles, crushed
1 | 10 cans (14 oz/400 g each) .	peeled plum tomatoes, drained of their juices
. . . .	Maldon sea salt and freshly ground black pepper
14 oz (400 g) | 9 lb (4 kg) . . .	penne
2 | 20	lemons, juiced
11 oz (300 g) | 6 lb 11 oz (3 kg) .	ricotta salata (salted, pressed ricotta), freshly grated
2 handfuls | 5 bunches	fresh marjoram, roughly chopped

In a heavy-bottom saucepan, cook the garlic in 3 tablespoons of the olive oil until it just begins to color. Add in the ginger and chiles, cook for a few minutes, and then stir in the drained tomatoes. Season with salt and pepper. Simmer over medium heat for 35 minutes until the tomatoes have broken up, stirring occasionally. Remove the tomatoes from the heat and pass them through a sieve or food mill.

Boil the penne in salted water until al dente. Drain and return to the pot. Add the remaining olive oil and the lemon juice to the penne and toss. Stir half the ricotta into the penne. Then mix in the tomato sauce and marjoram. Season to taste and serve with the remaining ricotta on the side.

A good vegetable stock is a staple of any vegetarian kitchen. In addition to this recipe, we use a number of variations in the studio, like our Shiitake Stock (see page 246) or our Kombu Stock (see page 321).

Vegetable Stock   Makes 3½ pints (2 liters)

3 medium	red onions, peeled and cut in quarters
3 medium	carrots, sliced
4 stalks	celery
a few stems	parsley
6	white peppercorns
2	bay leaves
2 cloves	garlic
1	lemon
3	small dry red chiles
1 medium	fennel

Any trimmed, leftover vegetable parts you may have can be used for the stock. Place the vegetables in a pot and cover with 3½ pints (2 liters) cold water. Bring to a boil, skimming off any foam as it surfaces. Lower the heat and simmer gently for 1 hour. Remove the bay leaves before serving.

Winter White Root Soup with Sage   Serves 6 | 60

¼ cup (60 g)	2⅓ cups (600 g)	butter
4 medium	9 lb (4 kg)	onions, diced
4 stalks	2 heads	celery, roughly chopped
1	7	small chiles, crushed
1	10 TB	dried sage
1	3 TB	dried thyme
	salt
a dash of	1¼ cups (300 ml)	white wine
9 oz (250 g)	5½ lb (2.5 kg)	celery root (celeriac), chopped
1 lb 2 oz (500 g)	11 lb (5 kg)	turnips (swede), chopped
9 oz (250 g)	5½ lb (2.5 kg)	parsnips, chopped
7 oz (200 g)	4½ lb (2 kg)	potatoes, peeled and chopped
1	10	bay leaves
¼	2 tsp	ground nutmeg
6¼ cups (1.5 liters)	4 gallons (15 liters)	Vegetable Stock (see above) or water
	freshly ground black pepper
a few stems	1 bunch	flat-leaf parsley, finely chopped

Melt the butter in a large heavy-bottom saucepan. Add the onions and gently cook over medium heat until they are soft and golden. Add the celery, chiles, sage, thyme, and some salt and continue to cook, stirring for 3 to 4 minutes to combine the flavors. Add the wine and cook for an additional 2 to 3 minutes. Add the celery root, turnips, parsnips, potatoes, bay leaves, nutmeg, and some salt. Add the vegetable stock or water, bring to a boil, and then reduce to medium heat and simmer for 40 minutes until the vegetables are tender. Turn off the heat, let cool slightly, and blend. Season with salt and pepper. Sprinkle with parsley and serve.

Winter White Root Soup
with Sage
see page 74

Tangy Chickpea Salad   Serves 6 | 60

1 can (14 oz/400 g) | 5½ lb (2.5 kg)	chickpeas, cooked and drained
1 handful | 14 oz (400 g)	golden raisins (sultanas)
1 handful | 14 oz (400 g)	almonds, roasted and chopped
2 stems | 2 bunches	scallions (spring onions), finely chopped
a few stems | 2 bunches	cilantro (coriander), chopped
1 | 6 clove/s	garlic, pressed
1 | 8	lemon/s, squeezed
2¼ oz (60 g) | 1 lb 5 oz (600 g) .	dried tomatoes in oil, chopped, oil reserved for dressing salad
1 tsp | ½ cup (125 ml)	olive oil
. . . .	salt and freshly ground black pepper

Combine all ingredients and mix well.

Poppy Seed Coleslaw   Serves 6 | 60

¼ | 3 medium head/s	white cabbage (around 4½ lb/2 kg each)
1 | 8 TB	poppy seeds
¼ tsp | 1 clove	garlic, crushed
1 tsp | 1 medium	lemon, juiced
2 TB | 1 cup (250 ml)	apple cider vinegar
4 TB | 2 cups (500 ml)	plain yogurt
¼ | 1 tsp	honey
¼ | 1 tsp	dijon mustard
a dash | 2 TB	soy sauce
¼ tsp | 3 TB	tahini
4 tsp | scant 1 cup (200 ml) . .	peanut oil
2 TB | 300 g	cashews, roasted
. . . .	salt and freshly ground black pepper

Thinly shred the cabbage by hand or in a food processor. For the dressing, whisk together poppy seeds, garlic, lemon juice, apple cider vinegar, yogurt, honey, mustard, soy sauce, tahini, and peanut oil. Just before serving, add the dressing to the cabbage and mix thoroughly with your hands. Add the cashews and season to taste with salt and pepper.

As with the Scones (see page 50), having fewer members at the Invalidenstrasse studio meant that it was possible to bake cookies for dessert after lunch. The studio was equipped with a clunky, temperamental electric cooker and a notoriously unreliable oven. A little bit of luck was needed to pull something out of it that wasn't either half-cooked or burned.

Still, it worked well enough that we could manage. Sometimes, it is only once you upgrade the kitchen that you finally realize the state of things you had been working with.

Now that the kitchen team has grown and we have a bigger oven, we are occasionally able to serve dessert after lunch again.

Chocolate-Hazelnut Cookies — Makes about 36 cookies

Amount	Ingredient
7 oz (200 g)	whole hazelnuts, roasted and coarsely chopped
2¼ cups (280 g)	all-purpose flour
½ tsp	baking powder (sodium bicarbonate)
1 tsp	salt
18 TB (250 g)	butter, softened
1 cup (220 g)	brown sugar
2 large	eggs
1 tsp	vanilla extract, powder (alternatively, 2 sachets of vanilla sugar)
7 oz (200 g)	dark chocolate, 60–70% cocoa, coarsely chopped

Preheat the oven to 400°F/200°C/Gas Mark 6. To toast the hazelnuts, spread them on a dry baking sheet (tray) and place in the oven for 5 to 10 minutes, until they begin to change color and the aroma fills the room. Remove from the oven and set aside until slightly cooled, then rub in a towel or between the palms of your hands to remove the skins. Chop coarsely.

Lower the oven temperature to 350°F/180°C/Gas Mark 4. Combine the flour, baking powder, and salt in a small bowl. With a wooden spoon or hand mixer, cream the butter until fluffy, then add the sugar. Add the eggs, one at a time, mixing well after each addition. Add the vanilla and combine. Add the dry ingredients and stir in the chocolate and the hazelnuts. If the dough seems too soft, refrigerate until firm. Drop teaspoons of dough on a lined baking sheet, leaving space on all sides to allow the cookies to spread (a dollop of dough will spread up to three times its size). Bake in the oven for 8 to 10 minutes, until golden. Don't overbake – the cookies should be chewy in the middle. Check often as the cookies can easily burn.

Variations
The hazelnuts can be substituted with any nuts or dried fruit. Fine oats can also be added (if using, reduce the amount of flour proportionally). Other variations include white chocolate, sesame, and cranberry; dark chocolate, white chocolate, oats, and walnuts; white chocolate and cashews; or dark chocolate with mixed nuts and raisins.

We usually serve two large pots for lunch, each one with a different variation of risotto. This risotto pairs particularly well with the Chicory with Fennel and Tarragon variety.

Tuscan Kale Risotto with Mushrooms and Rosemary   Serves 6 | 60

a few leaves | 4 large bunches	Tuscan kale
4 TB | 1¼ cups (300 ml)	olive oil
. . . .	salt and pepper
⅓ cup (75 ml) | 1 bottle (750 ml) .	dry white wine
7 oz (200 g) | 4½ lb (2 kg) . . .	mushrooms, cleaned
1 tsp | 2 bunches	fresh rosemary, finely chopped
1 tsp | 14 oz (400 g)	mascarpone (optional)
6¼ cups (1.5 liters) | 4 gallons (15 liters)	Vegetable Stock (see page 74)
3 TB (50 g) | 1 lb 2 oz (500 g) . .	butter
2 medium | 9 lb (4 kg)	onions, diced
½ head | 5 heads	celery, finely chopped, leaves kept separate
1 lb 5 oz (600 g) | 13.5 lb (6 kg)	brown arborio rice
7 oz (200 g) | 4½ lb (2 kg) . . .	parmesan, grated

Trim the kale and cut the leaves from the ribs. Chop both and keep separate. Cook the ribs in a bit of olive oil until they are soft and the pan is dry. Add the leaves, salt, pepper, and a little white wine and cover the pan. Set aside. Tear or chop the mushrooms and cook them in olive oil with salt, pepper, and rosemary. If desired, stir in mascarpone for a creamier mixture.

Heat the stock and check for seasoning. In a large pot, melt the butter and gently cook the onions and celery stalks until browned. Add the celery leaves, stir to combine, and then add the rice. Stir to coat each grain. The rice should become translucent. Add the wine and cook until absorbed, stirring constantly. Begin to add the hot stock, ladle by ladle, stirring throughout and allowing each ladle to be absorbed by the rice before adding the next. Continue until the rice is al dente, about 30 to 40 minutes. Add the prepared vegetables and herbs along with the parmesan, a bit of butter, and, if needed, some additional stock. Stir until everything is well combined. Cover, turn off the heat, and let sit for 5 minutes. Uncover, stir again, and season with salt and pepper. You may need to add a little more stock to achieve the desired consistency. Serve hot with a simple green salad on the side.

Variations
Chicory with Fennel and Tarragon – cook chicory and fennel separately in olive oil until al dente. Add freshly chopped tarragon at the end and salt and pepper to taste.
Red Kuri Squash – seed and cut the squash into 3 cm chunks. Oven roast with olive oil, salt and pepper, chiles, and thyme. Add at the end with parmesan and freshly chopped parsley.
Radicchio – cook with olive oil, lots of rosemary, salt, pepper, and a splash of balsamic vinegar. Add at the end with parmesan and fresh parsley.
Beet and Swiss chard – bake the beets, peel, and slice in rounds. Then halve the rounds. Ahead of time, cook the Swiss chard in white wine with salt and pepper and lemon zest.

Cooking Up Breaking Down, School and Art and Metabolisms

Eric Ellingsen and Christina Werner, codirectors,
Institut für Raumexperimente

The Institut für Raumexperimente (Institute for Spatial Experiments) is a big intricate digestive system that tries to choreograph in-feelings, a state of being inside of feeling, like feeling is a place, has a shape, is habitable, like a garden or pavilion is habitable. "In-feeling" is one way to translate the German *Einfühlung,* usually translated as empathy. In-feeling is a kind of stove in the body kitchen. It is a way of touching. In the school we plant the content together. We are kitchening. Things are cooking. One of the ways we do this is through food experiments. These experiments are coupled into workshops and larger teaching experiments the institute twists together, often in the format of three-day-long marathons centered around a specific theme.

Our favorite recipe in the institute is to not use recipes. We feel our way around. As scientist and biologist Donna Haraway says, we are companions. And the Latin root of companions, *cum panis,* means "with bread." We break bread together. We loaf around together. To be companions is not a passive thing. It is nourishing. Eating becomes us. Eating roots becomes us, even the Latin type. Breaking bread together has been a central core to growing the institute's content. Eating together is something meticulously choreographed to allow the unplanned to take place. The eating experiments are interior to the content of the teaching experiments. Content is seeded, not handed out like a preprocessed meal. The experiments are designed so that as they grow, branches which are not predesigned can design themselves. The informal can emerge. Breaking bread together helps those in the institute think about what we are serving each other in terms of learning, health, feelings, ideas, critique, and art. Breaking bread helps us to experience something together and reflect on our different tastes from the same thing. It allows a sameness that scoops different.

Over the years, the kitchen team has conducted and been involved in several food experiments in connection with a number of marathons. These collaborations between people, relationships, institutions, budgets, and timing are intersecting lines that curve into and across one another along the trajectory of the institute's and kitchen's everydayness. Some of these collaborations originate from the thinking seeds and needs of the institute, from workshops and people with whom the institute has some larger landscape moving through the school's curriculum and content. The meals that we make together around the kitchen are spirals. The lines we are, are curves. And the spaces we make in overlapping are not static territories but spatial relationships that move students across Berlin to meet in an institute above an art studio above and below a kitchen. We heat these spaces by moving through them, a teaspoon of this, a cup of that — a lot of pinches meeting in a bowl.

On the way to and from the kitchen we bowl. We are literally walking through a studio practice that practices, a practice of different landscapes and projects, of works and makings, lamps, pavilions, lights, books, buildings, friendships, frustrations, and exhibitions. We collect these impressions together into a buffet of feelings and ideas; our rhythms and thoughts are buffeted by these kitchen and studio practices whether we are conscious of it or not. Another metabolism is at work in the work, another breaking things down, another adding up. To sit at lunch tables around these productions is to be set in the space of things present and on their way. To be on the way is a place of presence too, then. All food is an on-the-way made up of ingredients, microbes, love, machinery, technique, tradition, things that are on their way to becoming us, on their way to becoming earth again. How do we metabolize a space for ideas and differences and cares we have in common? How do we metabolize a precise artwork from a bowl of ideas for an art practice? How do we cook a precise teaching experiment from a field of growing ideas?

Perhaps learning is a process of what we might remember, and a healthy school, a garden that is aware of constantly being cultivated to re/member itself. We are history re/membering history, re/membering philosophy, re/membering artworks. We re/member that art works. To re/member anything is to break it apart. Not to decon-

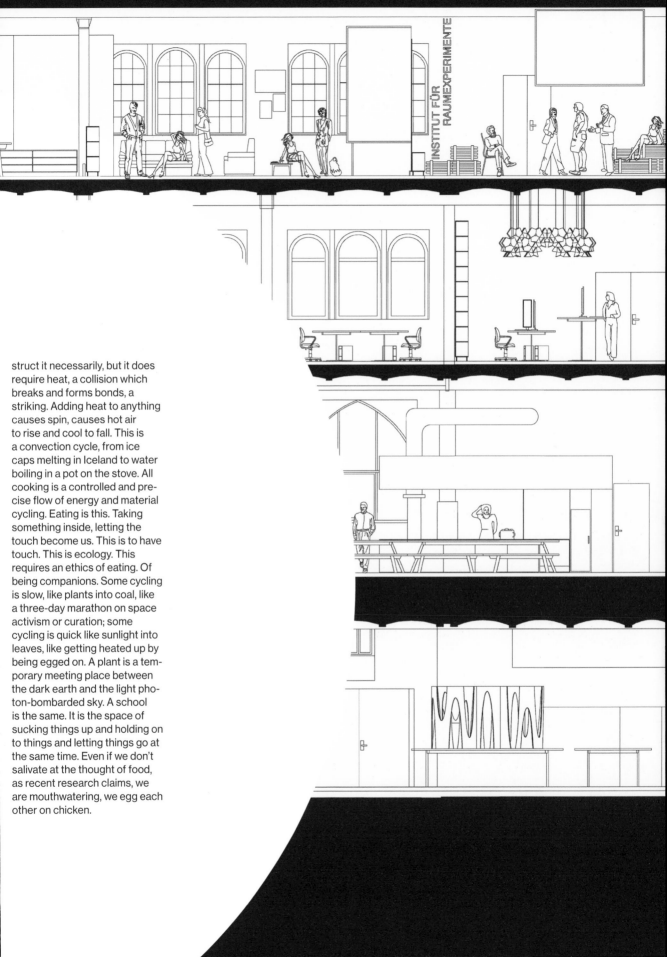

INSTITUT FÜR RAUMEXPERIMENTE

struct it necessarily, but it does require heat, a collision which breaks and forms bonds, a striking. Adding heat to anything causes spin, causes hot air to rise and cool to fall. This is a convection cycle, from ice caps melting in Iceland to water boiling in a pot on the stove. All cooking is a controlled and precise flow of energy and material cycling. Eating is this. Taking something inside, letting the touch become us. This is to have touch. This is ecology. This requires an ethics of eating. Of being companions. Some cycling is slow, like plants into coal, like a three-day marathon on space activism or curation; some cycling is quick like sunlight into leaves, like getting heated up by being egged on. A plant is a temporary meeting place between the dark earth and the light photon-bombarded sky. A school is the same. It is the space of sucking things up and holding on to things and letting things go at the same time. Even if we don't salivate at the thought of food, as recent research claims, we are mouthwatering, we egg each other on chicken.

II Body

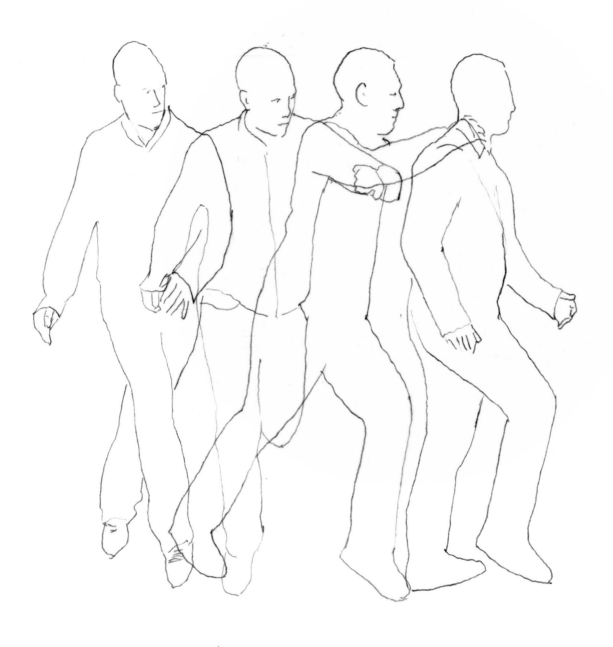

Body

Asako Iwama and
Lauren Maurer

To know what to cook, we have to listen to our bodies. We are constantly confronted by all kinds of messages telling us what to eat, but our bodies already know what we need. We just have to rediscover this, to sense it. Our bodies are composed of a variety of elements. About 60 percent of the human body is water: it is the solvent in which the reactions that make up our metabolism take place. Carbohydrates are our bodies' key source of energy. Proteins contribute to the building of cells. Lipids provide energy. Nucleic acids (in the form of DNA and RNA) hold the body's genetic information. We also share our bodies with countless microorganisms living within us. In a healthy body, this relationship is in balance and highly productive. It helps the digestion and the breaking down of nutrients to fuel the metabolism.

When we think about food, we ask ourselves how to feed this body, how to keep it in balance. These questions guide us in choosing organic, seasonal ingredients that provide us with the energy we need. But we don't just ask what nutrients the body needs; we also consider its senses to guide us in choosing the food we eat. There was a time when the senses were the primary tool for differentiating between beneficial and potentially poisonous substances; crucial instruments for making this vital distinction were the olfactory and the gustatory senses – smell and taste. While we still have the ability to differentiate, today we have to cultivate our senses to (re)learn how to use the bandwidth of experiences that condition our individual appetite and preferences. With trained senses, we may realize that our appetites often have more to do with what is good for our organism than we think. The apparent dislike of a food may point to an intolerance. We should connect with our senses, listen to what they tell us, trust our instincts. In cooking, we hope to find a balance between an awareness of the ingredients and the body – to translate appetite into a choice of healthy foods that nourish us.

Olafur Eliasson
Still from *Your embodied garden,*
2013

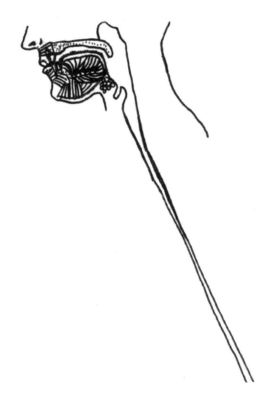

~

Taste

Pireeni Sundaralingam, poet and cognitive scientist

With a skin surface covered in over a quarter of a million taste buds, catfish have been described by researchers as "swimming tongues"; they have the ability to taste their entire environment.*

Bored by the flavor of your clothes,
you shed them and taste wind, ice,
the cocktail of fluids that spills from the sky.
Each building becomes a pool,
an aquarium of salt and sweat, atoms
of other lives cascading down the steps.
Your skin hungers, gasps. The air currents
bring news from each shy corner of the room.
and you taste and taste and taste:
leather, plastic, steel, the fist
of the raw doorknob,
the knife gripped between your hands.

* John Caprio et al., "The Taste System of the Channel Catfish: From Biophysics to Behavior," *Trends in Neurosciences* 16, no. 5, May 1993, pp. 192–97.

Olafur Eliasson
Seu caminho sentido, 2011

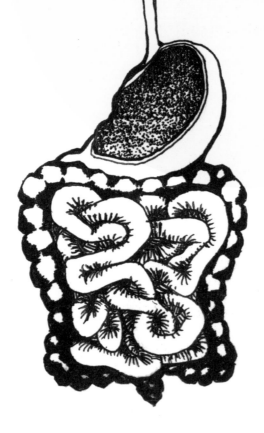

"The act of eating is not merely about burning calories and producing energy, but is in fact about replacing each individual part of your body . . . The flow of food . . . starts when it was harvested and continues as it is stored, cooked, fermented, chewed in the mouth, and digested. In other words, the act of eating, seen from both the perspective of body and the perspective of food, is inseparable from the flow of time . . ."

‖ Fukuoka Shin-Ichi ‖
Diet and Life: For Humans
to Become People

A rare exception to the studio's vegetarian cooking: In the summer, studio members sometimes fire up grills made in the workshop and load them with a variety of organic meats and vegetables. Here, in the garden of the Invalidenstrasse studio, 2008

Barbecue at Pfefferberg, 2013

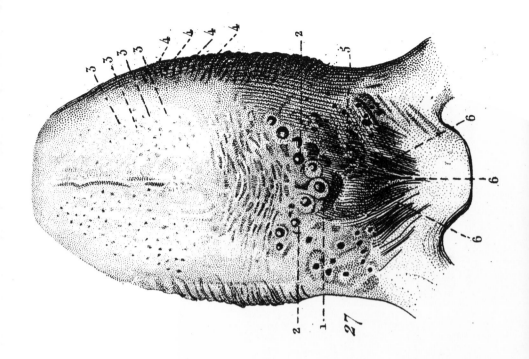

"[M]an evolved from unicellular organisms that appeared on the Earth about 3 billion years ago. The evolution of man passed through the stages of fish, amphibian, carnivorous animal, fruitarian ape, grain-eating ape, and finally to modern man . . . In our daily life, we eat two or three times a day, or even five times. Whatever foods we eat, they are decomposed by the various digestive juices and are transformed into blood plasma in our intestinal walls. And then, later, this plasma is transformed into red cells and body cells. Another way to say it is that we are transmuting from vegetable to animal in twenty-four hours every day. In other words, the 3 billion years of evolution is taking place every day in our bodies."

‖ Herman Aihara ‖
‖ *The Spiralic Concept of Man* ‖

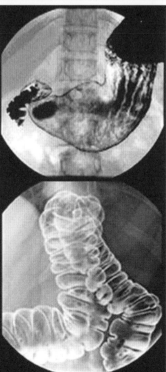

Top: Olafur Eliasson,
Your body as eye, 2009

Bottom left: Test for
Pedestrian vibes study, 2004

Bottom right: X-rays of a
human stomach and large
intestine

You Are Light

Tor Nørretranders, science writer and a frequent visitor of the studio

You are light. Sunlight. Pure shining light, absorbed by the living system on Planet Earth. You are light talking, light walking, and light eating light. Bright light, hungry light. Light.

All you eat is light. The energy comes from the sunlight. It is absorbed by plants and eaten by animals. But food is not just energy. It is also matter – just like you?

You are not matter. You are different. There is matter in you, but you are not the matter. You are something that matters. Think about it. You eat about 1 kilogram of matter each day. You drink something like 3 to 4 liters of matter in the form of various liquids. That adds up to around 4 kilograms of matter per day. In a year, it becomes more than one ton of matter, almost 1,500 kilograms. Yet your weight is likely to be less than 100 kilograms. You are just part of a huge flow of matter.

How long does the matter stay in you? It has been known for almost a century that the water molecules in you stay only for a few weeks. Then they are gone, just to be replaced by new ones. Your bones are made up of calcium, which stays around for months, but no more. In a year, 98 percent of the atoms in your body have been replaced. 98%!

If you are constant – having an identity throughout your life – it is not because you are the same material thing. You are not. All the stuff inside you changes all the time. It becomes shit, soil, flowers, cows, and thereby meat that you eat as food. So in the long run you become you again. You are you. So you are not matter. Or you would change all the time. You are something else.

You are a pattern in a flow. Your identity jumps all the time from atoms to atoms. The atoms in the food you had for lunch last month now form a pattern that help remembering your childhood. Your memories persist but the carrots and the cucumbers that carry them around – they change all the time.

The atoms jump and jump and jump between you and other inhabitants of the planet. And they jump into the atmosphere, the oceans, and the soil of the planet – and back again.

You are not matter. You are what matters. You are a pattern. A pattern in a flow of matter, driven by sunlight.

The pattern is made by sunlight, energized by sunlight, shaped by sunlight. But the pattern is not sunlight. The pattern is a pattern. You are a pattern. You are not sunlight. You are what sunlight does when it hits a planet.

You are not light. You are made by light. You are the way light shines through shit. You are the way dirt and soil rise up and make the light shine on.

Only stars can produce light. Only planets can produce you. You make the planet shine with light.

Thank you.

The Space Activism Marathon took place June 8–10, 2010 in the urban landscape of Berlin and at the Institut für Raumexperimente. The idea of the workshop was to uncover perspectives for the permanent and temporary use of urban space, and how understanding space and its usage can be a tool to make an impact on society. The institute's practitioners met with experts and peers from the fields of art, architecture, and urban planning, and with people engaged in diverse urban practices, such as BMX, parkour, street art, squatting, and free climbing. These encounters led to discussions of how space can be coproduced by the ways in which we engage in it. Another focus was on the interrelationships between surfaces, speeds of movement, and how art can choreograph these variables. On the first day of the marathon, lunch boxes accompanied the participants on their walks through Berlin; on the second day, only locally grown food was served; and, on the third day, only imported ingredients were used. Their spatial trajectory was visualized on food mile maps on the walls of the institute and in a small leaflet handed out to the participants. The experience of space also made its way into the body through the smell of food – transported from the kitchen on the ground floor to the participants gathering at the institute on the second floor.

Olafur Eliasson
Your mercury ocean, 2009

We are space life. We ear space life. We eat space for life. On the first day of the Space Activism Marathon, we walked around Berlin all day, coordinating with space activists – skateboarders, free climbers, parkour practitioners, and graffiti artists – all urban historians of squatting history. We wanted to feel where we were, so we performed walking experiments, which slowed us down while walking. This built up an appetite. We worked up our hunger. Then we worked with our hunger. As almost all foods these days come in on the fly, we wanted to make explicit these relationships and connections that we know in our mind, but sometimes don't taste on our palette. Sometimes, as Rilke says, "It takes wings to see the nearest things." Or it takes food. While walking through the city, small glass jars were prepared by the kitchen as lunch boxes. Each jar was a stratigraphy of warm and cool morsels. We turned a public space into a picnic place. We gathered in our attention and spread out our bodies. We tried to make explicit the systems we participate in, from food to urbanism to farms. During the second and third days, we organized the food so that guests would have to walk through the entire school to pick up a bowl and then walk through the space to fill the dish. Maps showed spatial and temporal distances between the ingredients and where we were then, extending to wherever you are eating these words now. All these things for a moment intersecting as soup, as seeds, as cells, as mouthfuls of breathing we shared like broth, and then acting together, and then spacing out somewhere else.

Eric Ellingsen and
Christina Werner

The ingredients for this lunch box were carefully selected for this event to create an even balance between textures, colors, and food types.

Pickled Eggs   Serves 6 | 60

6	50	dried shiitake mushrooms
3 TB	12 oz (300 g)	brown sugar
⅔ cup (150 ml)	1¾ pints (1 liter) .	soy sauce
2	12	star anise
1 thumb-	1 hand-sized piece . .	ginger, sliced
6	60	eggs, hard-boiled and peeled

Soak the dried shiitakes in water for 4 hours, until they soften. Put the brown sugar, 14 fl oz (400 ml) | 3½ pints (2 liters) water, soy sauce, anise, ginger, and shitake in a heavy-bottom saucepan and bring to a boil. Turn off the heat and let cool.

Place the hard-boiled eggs in the marinade and leave overnight, making sure to turn them occasionally so they color evenly. This dish also goes very well with ramen or rice.

Potato Croquettes   Serves 6 | 60

8 large	11 lb (5 kg)	potatoes
2 TB	18 TB (250 g)	butter
1	8 large	onion/s, chopped
. . . .	salt and freshly ground black pepper
2 TB	1⅔ cups (250 g)	all-purpose flour
1	8	egg/s, whisked
3 TB	14 oz (400 g)	bread crumbs
2¼ cups (500 ml)		
3½ pints (2 liters)	oil, for frying

Place the potatoes in cold water, bring to a boil, and cook until softened. Drain, peel off the skin while they are still hot, and mash.

Melt the butter in a heavy-bottom pan and gently fry the onions until caramelized. Mix together the onions with the potatoes and add salt and pepper to taste. Form 2-inch (5 cm) small balls. Turn them first in the flour, then in the eggs with a little water, and finally in the bread crumbs.

Pour the oil into a big saucepan to at least 2¾ inches (7 cm) deep and heat to between 180 and 350°F/185°C. Slip the croquettes, one at a time, into the hot oil. Fry until they are cooked on the inside and fox-colored brown on the outside, turning when necessary with a slotted spoon. Transfer onto paper towels to drain and serve immediately or keep warm for up to 30 minutes, uncovered, in an oven preheated to 200°F/100°C. Repeat the process with the remaining balls. Serve with Tomato Chile Sauce (see below).

Tomato Chile Sauce   Serves 6 | 60

scant ½ cup (100 ml)		
2¼ cups (500 ml)	olive oil
8 cloves	2 heads	garlic, minced
6	30	small dried red chiles, crushed
3	20 cans (14 oz/400 g each) .	tomatoes
. . . .	salt and freshly ground black pepper

Place the olive oil, garlic, and chiles in a heavy-bottom saucepan over medium heat. Cook for 1 or 2 minutes and add the tomatoes and a teaspoon of salt. Cook over medium heat for about 40 minutes, stirring often.

The sauce is done when the liquid is absorbed and the mixture has thickened. Use a wooden spoon to make a trail across the top, and make sure that no juice fills the trail. Season with salt and pepper.

Palak Paneer   Serves 6 | 60

1¾ pints (1 liter) | 10¾ pints (10 liters)	milk
½ | 4–5	lemon/s, juiced, plus more if needed
7 oz (200 g) | 4½ lb (2 kg) . . .	tofu
1 lb 2 oz (500 g) | 11 lb (5 kg) . .	spinach, washed and trimmed
3 TB | 1 lb 2 oz (500 g)	ghee (clarified butter) or sunflower oil, plus more as needed
2 medium | 6 lb 11 oz (3 kg) . . .	onions, diced
1½ TB | 3½ oz (100 g)	mustard seeds
2 | 7–10 cloves	garlic, minced
1 thumb- | 1 hand-sized piece . .	ginger, grated
3 | 30	small dried red chiles, crushed
1 tsp | 3 TB	cumin seeds
½ tsp | 1½ TB	coriander seeds, crushed
1 tsp | 2 TB	turmeric
1½ tsp | 5 TB	salt
2 | 24 cans (14 oz/400 g each) .	tomatoes
3½ (100 g) | 1 lb 5 oz (600 g) . .	cashews, finely ground
2 TB | 11 oz (300 g)	garam masala

Tofu marinade

1 TB | ⅔ cup (150 ml)	olive oil
½ tsp | 1½ TB	salt
1 | 10	small dried red chiles, crushed
½ tsp | 1½ TB	freshly ground black pepper

Also needed . . . . cheesecloth or a fine sieve

Preheat the oven to 400°F/200°C/Gas Mark 6. Ahead of time, make the paneer (Indian cottage cheese). Bring the milk to a boil, then add lemon juice. Boil until the milk has completely curdled and separated, adding more lemon juice if needed. Drain through the cheesecloth or a fine sieve. Allow the cheese to cool, placing a heavy object onto the cloth to drain any excess liquid.

Meanwhile, combine the marinade ingredients together. Slice the tofu into small rectangles and toss with the marinade. Place on a baking sheet (tray) and bake for 30 minutes.

Briefly blanch the spinach in plenty of salted boiling water until it is slightly undercooked, about 2 to 3 minutes. It should be a brilliant green color.

Drain well and purée in a food processor (work in batches for larger quantities).

Cut the paneer into small pieces, and, in a frying pan set over medium heat, fry in ghee or oil until golden brown and set aside.

Heat the ghee in a heavy-bottom saucepan and gently cook the onions until golden. Add the mustard seeds and cook until they pop. Add the garlic, ginger, chiles, cumin, coriander, turmeric, and salt, and fry over low heat until aromatic. Add the tomatoes and cashews, and simmer for 20 minutes over medium heat. Add the garam masala and spinach and cook for 10 minutes without a lid. Then add the paneer and tofu. Serve with basmati rice.

Sri Lankan Cauliflower Sambal   Serves 6 | 60

1 | 10 large	cauliflower/s (700 g each)
1 | 10 bunch/es	cilantro (coriander)
1 large | 3¼ lb (1.5 kg)	yellow onion
1 | 10	lemon/s
2 | 12	green chiles
2 TB | 10½ oz (300 g)	ghee (clarified butter) or vegetable oil
2 TB | 5½ oz (160 g)	black or yellow mustard seeds
1 TB | 1¼ oz (30 g)	fennel seeds
2 tsp | 2¼ oz (60 g)	cumin seeds
1 tsp | 4 TB	ground turmeric
1 tsp | 3 TB	ground cumin
1 tsp | 3 TB	chili powder
1 TB | 3½ oz (100 g)	ground coriander
1 tsp | 3 TB	salt
13 oz (375 g) | 6 lb 11 oz (3 kg) . .	desiccated (unsweetened) shredded coconut

By Pireeni Sundaralingam

Finely grate the cauliflower. This can take some time and is best done with the help of friends and alcohol. Coarsely chop the cilantro leaves and set aside. Finely dice the onion. Squeeze the lemon and set the juice aside. Cook the onions, together with green chiles, in ghee (or oil) until golden. Add mustard, fennel, and cumin seeds. Fry until the mustard seeds begin to pop. Add turmeric, ground cumin, chili powder, ground coriander, and

salt. Cook for 30 seconds. Add the cauliflower pieces. Stir and cook for 3 to 5 minutes, making sure that all the pieces are coated in the spices. Add the coconut. Mix thoroughly. Cook for another 5 minutes. Add cilantro leaves and lemon juice and mix. Serve immediately.

Best eaten as a side dish accompanying other curries and rice.

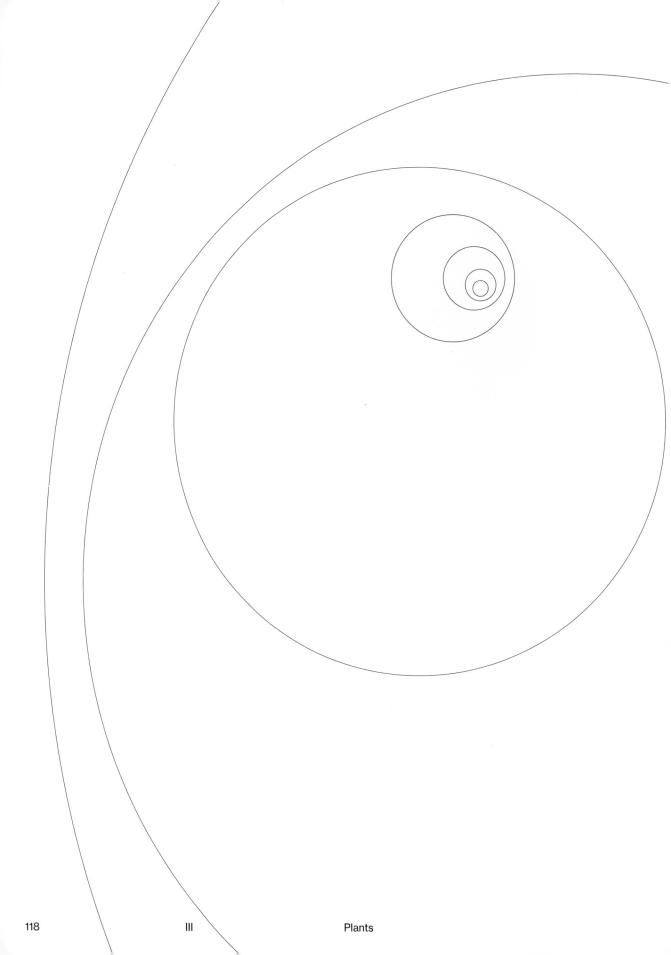

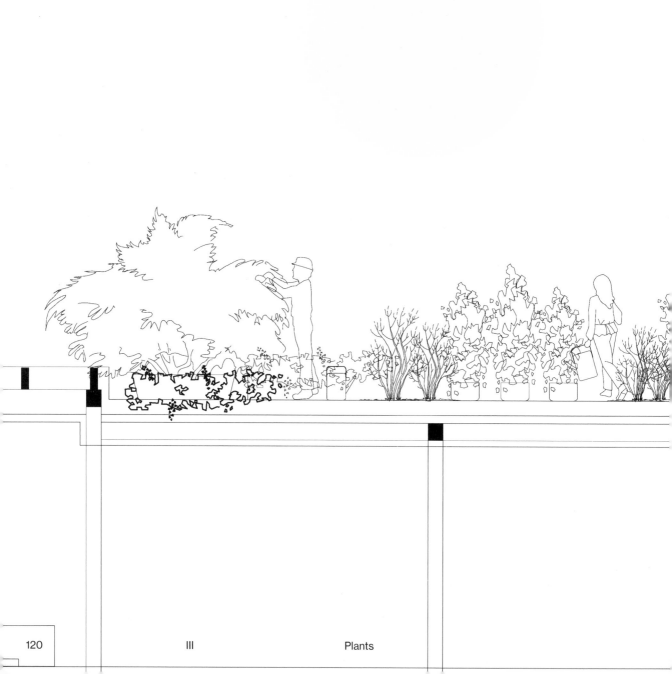

Plants

Asako Iwama and
Lauren Maurer

In the studio, we cook vegetarian dishes from locally grown, organic, or biodynamic fruit and vegetables. Cooking occurs not only in the kitchen, but across all stages of food preparation, so we have built up lasting collaborations with farmers and distributors. Much of our food is supplied by our longtime friends Anne Weis and Helmut Welp, who run an organic shop, called BioInsel, in the neighborhood of Schöneberg, Berlin. Some ingredients are grown, biodynamically, at Apfeltraum farm, just outside Berlin, and some are grown in our rooftop garden or in big planters in front of the windows of the kitchen.

Plants are one of the main nutritional sources for most animals,

including humans. Feeding on water and minerals, carbon dioxide and sunlight, plants undergo a cycle from seed to plant to fruit, and then to seed again. Before providing nutrition, they generate oxygen through photosynthesis. Without this process of translation, our bodies wouldn't understand the sun: to animals and humans, sunlight only proves life-sustaining once it has been transformed into edible energy.

Chlorophyll also plays a central role for the coloring of a plant. Like other pigments, it absorbs certain colors from the spectrum of light, causing the plant to appear a certain color to our eyes. While chlorophyll results in the color green, carotenoids

produce yellow, orange, or red; betalains create yellow, and anthocyanins yield bluish-red tones. Cutting a fruit or vegetable in half, a stunning array of colors is revealed, but also – over and over again – a circular shape, reflecting a spiral pattern of growth. The spiral is a strong image that conveys the idea of a constant energy flow, spiraling up and down, from the earth into the universe. It is something we see reflected in time and space in the growth from seed to plant, in the acts of harvesting, cooking, and eating, in digestion, decay, and regrowth.

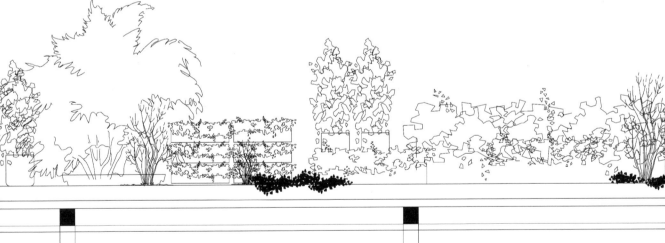

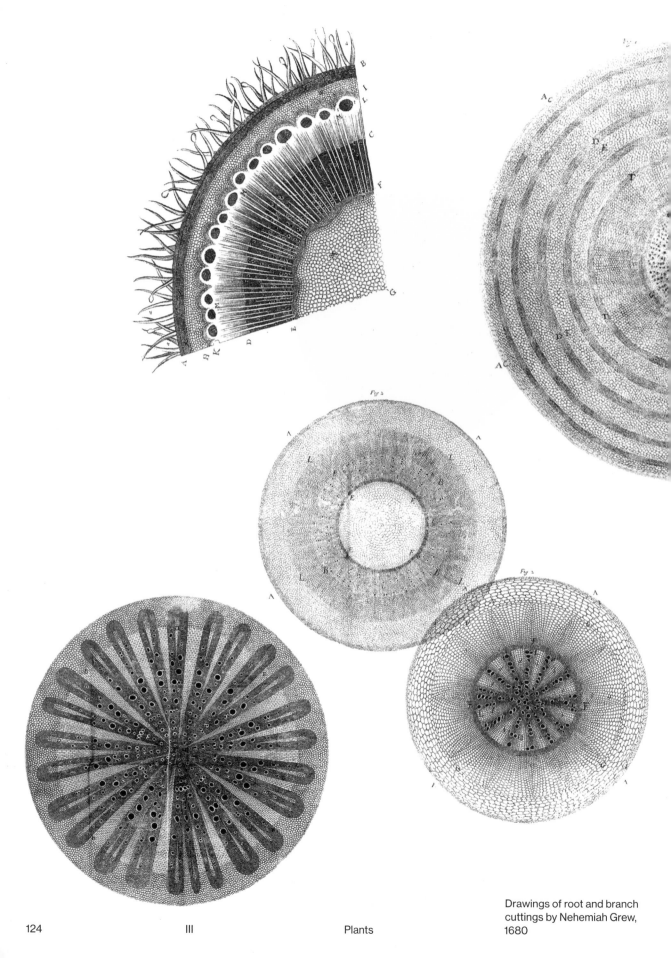

III

Plants

Drawings of root and branch
cuttings by Nehemiah Grew,
1680

From Wilhelm Troll's illustrations
of Johann Wolfgang von Goethe's
The Metamorphosis of Plants

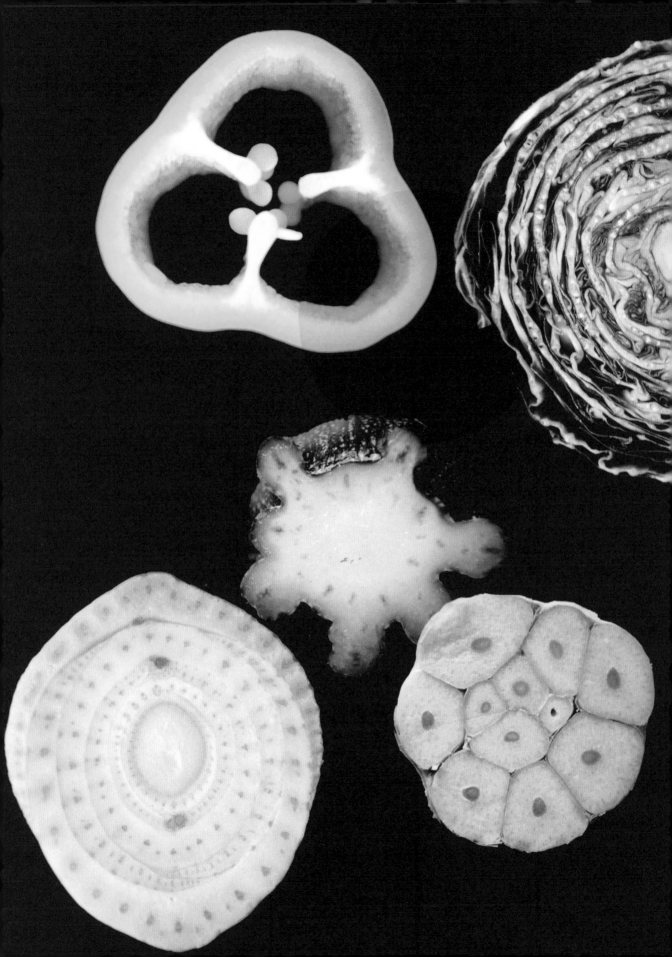

PLANT

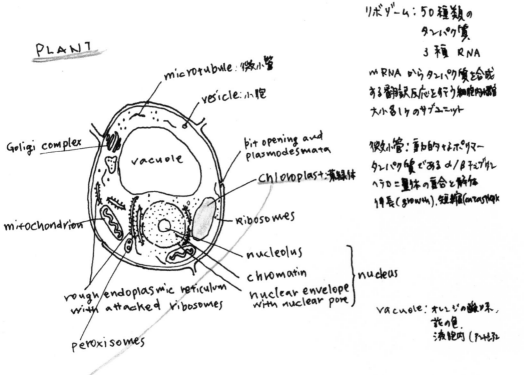

リボゾーム：50種類の
タンパク質
3種 RNA

mRNA からタンパク質を合成
する翻訳反応を行う細胞内器官
大小1ケのサブユニット

微小管：動的なポリマー
タンパク質である α/β チュブリン
ヘテロ二量体の重合と解体
伸長 (growth)、短縮 (anastrophe)

Plant cell labels:
- microtubule: 微小管
- vesicle: 小胞
- Goligi complex
- vacuole
- pit opening and plasmodesmata
- Chloroplast: 葉緑体
- mitochondrion
- Ribosomes
- nucleolus
- chromatin
- nuclear envelope with nuclear pore
- } nucleus
- rough endoplasmic reticulum with attached ribosomes
- peroxisomes

vacuole：オレンジの酸味、
花の色、
液胞内（九州茶）

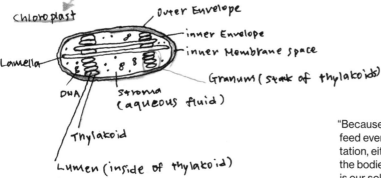

Chloroplast labels:
- Chloroplast
- Outer Envelope
- inner Envelope
- inner Membrane space
- Granum (stack of thylakoids)
- Lamella
- DNA
- Stroma (aqueous fluid)
- Thylakoid
- Lumen (inside of thylakoid)

"Because animals, including man, feed eventually on green vegetation, either directly or through the bodies of other animals, it is our sole final source of nutriment. There is no alternative supply. Without sunlight and the capacity of the earth's green carpet to intercept its energy for us, our industries, our trade, and our possessions would soon be useless. It follows therefore that everything on this planet must depend on the way mankind makes use of this green carpet, in other words on its efficiency."

|| Albert Howard
The Soil and Health: A Study of Organic Agriculture ||

Animal

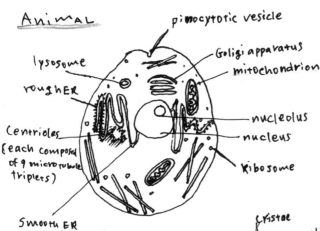

Animal cell labels:
- pinocytotic vesicle
- lysosome
- Goligi apparatus
- mitochondrion
- rougher
- nucleolus
- nucleus
- Centrioles (each composed of 9 microtubule triplets)
- Ribosome
- Smooth ER (no ribosome)

Mitochondrion labels:
- cristae
- inner boundary membrane
- cristal membrance
- Ribosome
- Matrix Granule
- Mitochondrial DNA

Drawings of plant and animal cells and notes by Asako Iwama

The weekly food delivery
from BioInsel

~~~~~~~~~~

Water me / Eat me

Anne Duk Hee Jordan,
participant in the Institut für
Raumexperimente

2012
potato skin, copper, zinc
C-print, 11.7×16.5 in (29.7×42 cm)

The potatoes photographed
here have traveled through
an entire lifespan. I first grew
potato cuttings, feeding them
with my own blood via infusions.
Then I planted the potatoes
and linked them together with
wire to create a biological circuit.
The energy from the potato
circuit drove a watering machine, which kept the potatoes
hydrated. Thus, the energy of
the potatoes was redirected
into their own self-contained,
natural circuit, driving the motor
that supplied them with nutrients
and promoted their growth. As
the potatoes grew into adults,
they contributed more energy
to the development of the
younger ones, linking the beginning and end of life through the
same system. When the older
potatoes died, I buried them in
the soil and kept their skin.

 Plants

We took advantage of the many surfaces and niches around the Pfefferberg studio to begin our own vegetable garden. When we started growing plants on the rooftop in 2009, the roof could only be accessed through a small crawl space in the tower of the main stairwell. We nearly risked our lives hauling the soil needed for all the planters out through the passageway. The first year, our crop included tomatoes, beans, zucchini, carrots, chiles, squash, and lots of herbs.

After herbs, tomatoes were the only produce that could be grown on the rooftop garden in enough mass to supply the whole studio for lunch. For three years, we grew heirloom tomatoes from seeds we received from Apfeltraum farm.

Caring for the garden was a daily chore, usually done in the morning before the temperature grew too hot. It was windy up on the roof, so Thórdís Magnea Jónsdóttir, an architect and former member of the kitchen team, built a system to stabilize the tomato plants.

Tomato Secco
(see page 353)

"Each cell in the interior of a green leaf contains minute specks of a substance called chlorophyll and it is this chloro- phyll which enables the plant to grow. Growth implies a continu- ous supply of nourishment. Now plants do not merely collect their food: they manufacture it before they can feed. In this they differ from animals and man, who search for what they can pass through their stomachs and alimentary systems, but cannot do more; if they are un- able to find what is suitable to their natures and ready for them, they perish. A plant is, in a way, a more wonderful instrument. It is an actual food factory, mak- ing what it requires before it begins the processes of feeding and digestion."

Albert Howard
The Soil and Health: A Study of Organic Agriculture

Artist Marathon

The Artist Marathon took place December 8–11, 2009, at the Institut für Raumexperimente. Thirty-four artists who live in Berlin presented their works, discussed artistic ideas and approaches, and shared their experiences and interests in the production of spatial reality. As a way of building the event's rhythm, the artists were grouped according to a color code devised to represent their different practices, topics, or media.

The food concept reflected this color system: one day, lunch consisted only of white dishes; another day, all dishes were pink; and on other days, they were green or orange. This made explicit the flow and immersion of colors that enter the body through the act of eating, encouraging the participants to think, *"I'm eating orange,"* instead of *"I'm eating carrots."* The food experiments were accompanied by a small specially made leaflet by Asako Iwama, Lauren Maurer, and Jules Gaffney.

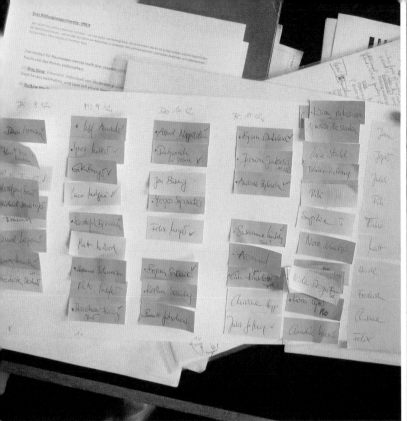

Color in food is brought into our body by first being placed in our mouth. It swells on our tongue and between our teeth. Color flows down our throat and esophagus into our stomach, which mixes in acids. The small intestine has enzymes and the large intestine has bacteria that finish breaking color down.
In this way, color blends through and is integrated into our body.

Asako Iwama, Lauren Maurer, and Jules Gaffney, former member of the studio team

Sound-visualizing experiment by studio member Matt Willard

145

The dishes prepared in conjunction with the Artist Marathon were organized by color, so that when taken together, the food represented a wide spectrum of pigments, with one color served each day.

Marinated Red and Yellow Peppers with Capers   Serves 6 | 60   Adapted from *The River Café Cookbook*

6 medium	5½ lb (2.5 kg)	red bell peppers
6 medium	5½ lb (2.5 kg)	yellow bell peppers
2 cloves	2 heads	garlic, sliced
1¾ oz (50 g)	1 lb 2 oz (500 g)	salted capers
2 TB	2 bunches	marjoram, finely chopped
	freshly ground black pepper
	extra virgin olive oil, for drizzling
	bread, for serving

Preheat the oven to 475°F/250°C/Gas Mark 9. Roast the peppers in the oven until their skin is charred. Remove from the oven and let sit until cool enough to handle. Remove the blackened skin, core, and seeds. Over the top of the peppers, sprinkle garlic, capers, marjoram, and pepper. Drizzle with olive oil and serve with some nice, crusty bread.

Green Curry Paste   Makes ¾ cup (175 ml)   Adapted from *The Dean and DeLuca Cookbook*

3 tsp	coriander seeds
2 tsp	cumin seeds
1 tsp	black or white peppercorns
2	shallots or small onions, chopped
5–15 small	green chiles, coarsely chopped
3 stalks	lemongrass, thinly sliced
2 TB	ginger, minced
1 TB	garlic, minced
6 TB	cilantro (coriander) roots, stems, and leaves, chopped
8	kaffir lime leaves, chopped
3 tsp	lime zest
	fresh lime juice
	coarse salt

In a large mortar, crush the coriander, cumin seeds, and peppercorns. Add in the shallots, chiles, lemongrass, ginger, and garlic and pound into a paste. Pound in the chopped cilantro roots, stems, and leaves as well as the lime leaves, zest, and juice until a smooth paste forms. Add salt to taste (alternatively, umesu can be used, if you have it). The curry paste may be stored in an airtight container in the fridge for a few weeks.

For the Artist Marathon, we used this paste in a basic curry with broccoli, zucchini, green peppers, and tofu.

The original recipe calls for fish sauce or shrimp paste, but we do not use either, because they tend to contain a lot of MSG and contribute to overfishing.

Flan with Caramel Sauce   Serves 6

For the caramel sauce

2 cups (400 g)	sugar
a pinch	salt
¼ cup (60 ml)	cold water
⅔ cup (160 ml)	boiling water

For the flan

. . . .	butter, for greasing
1	vanilla bean pod
1¾ cups plus 2 TB (400 ml) . .	milk
¾ cup plus 1 TB (200 ml) . . .	heavy (double) cream
3½ oz (100 g)	sugar
4	eggs
1	egg yolk

Preheat oven to 350°F/180°C/ Gas Mark 4. To make the caramel sauce, place the sugar, salt, and ¼ cup (60 ml) cold water in a heavy-bottom saucepan over medium heat. As the mixture begins to simmer, allow it to turn brown without stirring. Be careful not to let it burn. Add ⅔ cup (160 ml) boiling water and stir. Remove from the heat and strain into the baking dish to cool.

To make the flan, butter the edges of the now-cooled baking dish. Cut the vanilla pod in half and scrape out the beans. Combine the milk, cream, sugar, and vanilla beans in a pan and cook over low heat to melt the sugar. Put the eggs and egg yolk in a bowl and mix well. Slowly add the egg to the milk mixture, stirring constantly. Do not let it boil. Pour the mixture carefully through a sieve into the prepared dish. Place the dish into a high-walled pan filled with water to create a water bath. Bake for 50 to 60 minutes. Remove the flan from the oven, and its water-bath, and let it cool completely. Gently remove it from the baking dish by first running a knife around the inside edges of the dish, and then placing a serving dish upside down on top of the baking dish and carefully turning it over. The flan tastes even better when prepared in advance and refrigerated overnight.

Brussels Sprouts and Baked Ricotta   Serves 6 | 60

1 lb 2 oz (500 g)	11 lb (5 kg) . .	Brussels sprouts, trimmed
9 oz (250 g)	6 lb 11 oz (3 kg) . .	ricotta
. . . .	olive oil, for drizzling
1	10	small dried red chile/s
. . . .	sea salt and freshly ground black pepper
½	5 TB	thyme

Preheat the oven to 425°F/ 220°C/Gas Mark 7. Boil the Brussels sprouts in salted water for 8 minutes and set aside. Line a baking sheet (tray) with parchment (baking) paper and place the ricotta on it. Drizzle with olive oil and bake until lightly browned. Take the ricotta out of the oven, crush down with a fork, and sprinkle with olive oil, chiles, salt, and pepper. Place back into the oven and mix from time to time with a fork. Put the Brussels sprouts in a baking dish, drizzle with olive oil, thyme, and salt and bake for 30 minutes until golden. Gently mix the sprouts with the ricotta and sprinkle with pepper.

Mixed Rice

We often cook brown short-grain rice, basmati rice, or barley and mix it with chili (page 278), curry (page 158), or ratatouille (page 281) from the previous day, adding some spices, fresh herbs, sliced pepper or zucchini, and roasted nuts or sesame seeds to make a new rice dish. Grate cheese over the top and place the dish in the oven for a baked variation.

This can be paired with many different dishes or as part of an antipasti plate. Try with Brussels Sprouts and Baked Ricotta (see above), Baked Chicory (see page 196), Pressed Salad and Baked Beets with Horse-radish Dill Almond Sauce (see page 49), or Pinto Beans with Kohlrabi, Radishes, and Fresh Cilantro (see page 200).

Baked Chicory
see page 196

Tomato Soup with Cumin and Figs   Serves 6 | 60

scant ½ cup (100 ml) |
   1¾ pints (1 liter) . . . . . . olive oil
2 medium | 5½ lb (2.5 kg) . . . onions, chopped
¾ cup (200 ml) | 1 bottle (750 ml) white wine
1 large | 4½ lb (2 kg). . . . . red bell pepper/s, chopped
1 | 10 TB . . . . cumin seeds, lightly roasted
   and crushed
2 | 15 cans (14 oz/400 g each) tomatoes
5 oz (150 g) | 3¼ lb (1.5 kg) . . dried figs, chopped
2¼ lb (1 kg) | 22 lb (10 kg) . . fresh tomatoes, roughly
   chopped
. . . . sea salt and freshly ground
   black pepper
5 or 6 large | 5½ lb (2 kg) . . . fresh figs, finely diced

Adapted from *Moro East*

Heat the olive oil in a heavy-bottom saucepan. Cook the onion with a good pinch of salt over medium heat. Add the wine and cook until evaporated. Add the red peppers and continue cooking until softened. Stir in the cumin, then add the canned tomatoes and dried figs and let simmer for about 1 hour, stirring occasionally. When the mixture has reduced, put in the fresh tomatoes and increase the heat slightly, simmering for 15 minutes. Blend until smooth, adding olive oil and water, as necessary, until creamy. Season well with salt and pepper. Serve with the fresh figs sprinkled on top.

Broccoli and Barley with Parsley   Serves 6 | 60

3½ oz (100 g) | 2¼ lb (1 kg) . . . barley
¼ cup (70 ml) | 3 cups (700 ml) . olive oil
1 | 7 bunches . . . . flat-leaf parsley, minced
2 cloves | 1 head . . . . garlic, crushed
. . . . sea salt and freshly ground
   black pepper
2 | 15 heads . . . . broccoli, flowers and stalks
   trimmed
3½ oz (100 g) | 2¼ lb (1 kg) . . . feta, crumbled (optional)

By Montse Torredà Martí,
member of the kitchen team and film department

Soak the barley in cold water for 30 minutes. Meanwhile, mix together the olive oil, parsley, garlic, salt, and pepper and set aside. Using the soaking water, boil the barley for about 30 minutes, or until al dente. Drain and set aside. Blanch the broccoli for 3 to 5 minutes so that it stays crunchy. Combine the broccoli, barley, and dressed parsley, and taste for seasoning. Add the feta.

For one of Olafur's birthdays, a number of studio members brought in their favorite cake recipes and prepared them in the kitchen. This carrot cake was one of the most popular and remains an all-time favorite.

Carrot Cake Serves 12

For the cake

. . . .	butter, for greasing
2¼ cups (280 g)	all-purpose flour
2 tsp.	baking powder (sodium bicarbonate)
1 tsp	salt
¾ cup (175 ml)	sunflower oil (or 10 TB/150 g melted butter)
1 cup plus 2 TB (250 g)	brown sugar
3	eggs
4 medium	carrots, finely grated
7 oz (200 g)	fresh pineapple chunks, drained
5 oz (150 g)	walnuts, chopped
1½ tsp	cinnamon
1 tsp	vanilla extract (or 2 packs vanilla sugar)

For the frosting

14 oz (400 g)	cream cheese, at room temperature
3½ TB (50 g)	butter, melted
⅔–1 cup (75–100 g)	powdered (icing) sugar, sifted
2¾ oz (70 g)	finely shredded coconut (optional)
a little	milk or lemon juice

Preheat the oven to 350°F/180°C/Gas Mark 4. Lightly butter a Bundt pan. In a small bowl, whisk together the flour, baking powder, and salt and set aside. In a large bowl, whisk together the oil or butter and the brown sugar. Add the eggs and mix. Add the carrots, pineapple, walnuts, cinnamon, and vanilla and stir to mix. Add the flour mixture and stir until just combined. Pour into the baking pan and bake for 50 minutes. Test with a toothpick inserted – it should come out clean when done. Remove from the pan while still warm and let cool on a cake rack or plate. (If making muffins, the baking should take about 30 minutes.)

To make the frosting, beat the cream cheese with a hand mixer until soft. Slowly add the melted butter while mixing. Add the powdered (icing) sugar slowly, tasting often. When the frosting has reached the desired sweetness, add the coconut and, if needed, milk or lemon juice to achieve the desired spreading consistency. Frost the cake after it has cooled.

Variations
Leave out the carrots and pineapple and instead add one of these combinations: 3 large sour apples, cored and thinly sliced | 3 large zucchini, grated, drained, with zest of one lemon | 3 medium bananas, mashed with a fork | 2 small sweet potatoes, steamed and mashed | ½ red kuri squash or butternut squash, steamed and mashed, with 1 banana, mashed.

We first met Christina Kim, an artist and designer of sustainable and locally sourced fashion, during our trip to Chicago for the exhibition *Take your time: Olafur Eliasson* at the Museum of Contemporary Art. Christina made the tablecloths for the opening dinner. Later, when she traveled to Berlin, she visited Asako at home one evening and made this pasta for her.

Lemon Pasta   Serves 6 | 60

By Christina Kim

2 | 20 cloves	garlic, peeled
4 | 35	lemons, juiced and finely zested
. . . .	sea salt and freshly ground black pepper
1¾ oz (50 g) | 1 lb 2 oz (500 g) . .	pickled green peppers, chopped
generous ¾ cup (200 ml) | 6¼ cups (1.5 liters)	olive oil
7 oz (200 g) | 3¼ lb (1.5 kg) . . .	parmesan, freshly grated, plus extra for serving
600 g | 6 kg	spaghetti, or fusilli for the large quantity
2 handfuls | 8 bunches	basil or cilantro (coriander), finely chopped

In a mortar and pestle, pound together the garlic, zest, and salt. Add the pickled peppers and a dash of their juice and continue to pound. Season with pepper. Transfer to a large bowl, add the lemon juice and a generous amount of olive oil, and mix. Stir in the parmesan and set aside.

Cook the pasta in a generous amount of salted boiling water until al dente. Drain and add the pasta to the lemon sauce. Add the basil or cilantro, mix well, and serve with extra parmesan.

Fusilli with Green Beans, Roasted Potatoes, and Pesto   Serves 6 | 60

1 lb 2 oz (500 g) | 11 lb (5 kg) . .	potatoes, peeled and cubed
4 TB | 1¼ cups (300 ml)	olive oil
2 | 20	small chiles, crushed
. . . .	sea salt and freshly ground black pepper
10½ oz (300 g) | 6 lb 11 oz (3 kg) .	green beans, trimmed
21 oz (600 g) | 13 lb (6 kg) . . .	fusilli or other short pasta
5 oz (150 g) | 3½ lb (1.5 kg) . . .	Pesto Genovese (see page 188)
. . . .	Parmesan, grated

Preheat the oven to 400°F/ 200°C/Gas Mark 6. Toss the potatoes with olive oil, chiles, salt, and pepper and bake for about 20 minutes or until they are browned and some are crisp.

While the potatoes are in the oven, boil the beans in salted water for 5 minutes until tender but still crunchy. Drain, halve, and set aside.

Cook the pasta in a generous amount of salted boiling water until al dente, and then drain, reserving a little of the water. Return the pasta to the pot, and toss with the potatoes, green beans, pesto, and a few tablespoons of the pasta water, if needed. Add salt and pepper, and serve immediately with grated parmesan.

Massaman Curry   Serves 6 | 60

By Thomas Blumtritt-Hanisch,
member of the studio workshop team

1¾ pints (1 liter) | 2⅔ gallons (10 liters)	coconut cream
3 cups (750 ml) | 2 gallons (7.5 liters)	coconut milk
⅓ cup (70 ml) | 3 cups (700 ml) .	Massaman Curry Paste (see below)
7 | 70 small	new potatoes, peeled and quartered
3 | 30 small	sweet potatoes, peeled and cut into chunks
1 | 10	red kuri squash, cut into chunks
3½ oz (100 g) | 1 lb 3 oz (1 kg) . .	water chestnuts
5 | 50	very small onions or shallots
1 | 10 handful/s	pea eggplants (optional)
2 TB (30 ml) | 1¼ cup (300 ml) .	pineapple juice
4 TB | 14 oz (400 g)	palm sugar (or brown sugar or agave nectar)
2–3 TB | 1⅔ cup (400 ml) . . .	tamarind juice
3 TB | 1¾ cups (450 ml)	fish sauce (or ume su)
1 tsp | 3 TB	sea salt
3 TB | 9 oz (250 g)	peanuts, roasted
4 | 40	bay leaves, roasted
1½ tsp | 5 TB	cardamom seeds, roasted
1 | 15 stick/s	cinnamon, about 1 inch (3 cm) long
. . . .	fresh red spur chile slices or some sliced red pepper

In a large pot, bring the coconut cream and milk to a boil over medium heat. Place a heavy-bottom frying pan over medium heat. Skim two ladles of coconut oil from the pot and pour them into the pan. Once the oil is hot, spoon in the curry paste and fry gently until it is fragrant and the oil surfaces. Turn off the heat. Skim the surplus coconut oil from the pot with the coconut milk and cream and set aside. Pour the curry mixture from the frying pan into the pot of coconut milk.

Add the potatoes, sweet potatoes, and squash, and cook for about 15 minutes. Add the water chestnuts, onions or shallots, eggplant, and pineapple juice, and continue to cook for 10 more minutes.

Season to taste with palm sugar, tamarind juice, fish sauce, and sea salt. (For a vegetarian version, ume su can be substituted for the fish sauce. In this variation, use less tamarind juice, as the ume su is very salty and acidic.) The curry should have a balance of sweet, sour, and salty. Add the peanuts, bay leaves, cardamom seeds, and cinnamon and simmer until the vegetables are tender and the sauce has reduced slightly.

Ladle into a serving bowl and garnish with spur chiles. (Red pepper can be used instead of spur chiles for a milder curry.) Serve with rice on the side.

Massaman Curry Paste   Makes scant ½ cup (100 ml) | 3 cups (700 ml)

3 | 21	dried spur chiles, seeded and soaked until tender
1 | 7 tsp	sea salt
1 | 7 tsp	mature galangal, sliced and roasted
1 | 7 TB	lemongrass, sliced and roasted
2 | 14 heads	garlic, roasted and peeled
5 | 35	shallots, roasted and peeled
1 | 7 TB	coriander seeds, roasted and ground
1 | 7 pinch/es	cumin seeds, roasted and ground
2 | 14	cloves, roasted and ground
1 | 7 tsp	freshly ground black pepper
1 | 7 tsp	shrimp paste (optional)

In a mortar, finely pound the spur chiles and salt together. Add the galangal and lemongrass, pounding well. Add garlic, shallots, coriander seeds, cumin, cloves, pepper, and shrimp paste, if desired, and pound until a smooth paste forms. (If making more than you need for the curry, place the paste in a clean jar and refrigerate.)

Pressed Salad
with Lemon and Ume
see page 70

Volanti with Broccoli and Ricotta — Serves 6 | 60

1 lb 5 oz (600 g)	13 lb (6 kg) . .	broccoli, florets and trimmed stalks
1 medium	5½ lb (2 kg)	onion/s, diced
a pinch	1 TB	dried red chiles, ground
. . . .	olive oil
. . . .	sea salt and freshly ground black pepper
11 oz (300 g)	6⅔ lb (3 kg) . . .	ricotta
3½ oz (100 g)	2¼ lb (1 kg) . . .	kalamata olives, pitted
1 lb 5 oz (600 g)	13 lb (6 kg) . .	volanti pasta or any short pasta
. . . .	parmesan, grated

Blanch the broccoli for 8 minutes. Mash with a hand mixer. In a heavy-bottom pan, gently cook the onion and chiles in olive oil until caramelized. Add salt and pepper. Combine the broccoli, ricotta, olives, and onion mixture.

Cook the pasta in a generous amount of salted boiling water until al dente. Drain thoroughly, reserving a little of the water. Mix the pasta with the broccoli ricotta mixture, adding pasta water as needed. Serve topped with parmesan.

Marinated Tomatoes — Serves 6 | 60

6	60 small	tomatoes
1	10 medium	salad onion/s, finely sliced and rinsed
scant ½ cup (100 ml)	1 quart (1 liter)	white balsamic vinegar
½	5 tsp	sea salt

Bring a pot of water to a boil on the stove. Place a bowl of ice water next to the stove. Rinse and stem the tomatoes. Gently place the tomatoes into the boiling water and cook for about 1 minute, until the skin begins to split. (Do not boil too long or they will begin to soften and cook. If you have several tomatoes, boil them in batches of 3 to 4 at a time.)

Using a slotted spoon, transfer the tomatoes to the bowl with ice water, and let cool. This will stop the cooking process. Drain and peel the skin. Place tomatoes into a bowl with the onions, vinegar, and salt and refrigerate for at least 30 minutes, preferably overnight.

Creamy Pink Root Soup with Roasted Kohlrabi Serves 6 | 60

scant ½ cup (100 ml) | 2½ cups (600 ml)	olive oil, plus extra for drizzling
2 medium | 9 lb (4 kg)	onions, diced
2 cloves | 1 head	garlic, sliced
4 stalks | 4 heads	celery, diced
1 large | 4½ lb (2 kg).	red pepper/s, chopped
. . . .	sea salt and freshly ground black pepper
3½ TB (50 ml) | generous 2 cups (500 ml) . . .	white wine
8 medium | 13 lb (6 kg). . . .	beets, peeled and sliced
7 oz (200 g) | 4½ lb (2 kg) . .	potatoes, peeled and chopped
4 medium | 6 lb 11 oz (3 kg) . . .	carrots, sliced
3½ oz (100 g) | 2¼ lb (1 kg). . .	brown rice
2 | 10	bay leaves
6¼ cups (1.5 liters) | 4 gallons (15 liters)	Vegetable Stock (see page 74) or water
2 medium | 6 lb 11 oz (3 kg) . . .	kohlrabi or daikon, peeled and diced
. . . .	toasted pumpkin seeds
. . . .	roasted pumpkin seeds, for garnish

Heat the olive oil in a large, heavy-bottom saucepan and gently cook the onions over medium heat until they are golden. Add the garlic, celery, red peppers, and a pinch of salt and continue to cook until soft, stirring to combine the flavors. Add the wine and cook until evaporated. Add the beets, potatoes, carrots, brown rice, bay leaves, and some salt. Cover with the stock or water, and bring to a boil. Reduce heat to medium and simmer for 40 minutes, until the vegetables are done. While the soup is cooking, cook the kohlrabi until tender and set aside. Turn off the heat, and after the soup has cooled slightly, blend. Add the kohlrabi, taste for salt, and season with pepper. Drizzle with olive oil and sprinkle toasted pumpkin seeds on top. (Alternatively, you can serve the soup with sour cream or crème fraîche and chopped parsley.)

Zucchini Filled with Ricotta and Marjoram Serves 6 | 60

6 medium | 13 lb (6 kg)	zucchini, halved across
1 TB (15 g) | 10 TB (150 g). . .	butter
2¼ oz (60 g) | 1 lb 5 oz (600 g) .	feta, crumbled
1¾ oz (50 g) | 1 lb 2 oz (500 g). .	ricotta or cottage cheese
2¼ oz (60 g) | 1 lb 5 oz (600 g) .	gruyère, grated
1 | 7	egg/s
2 tsp | 6 TB	fresh marjoram, chopped
1 tsp | 3 TB	all-purpose flour
. . . .	sea salt and freshly ground black pepper
2 tsp | 6 TB	flat-leaf parsley, chopped

Preheat the grill or oven to 350°F/180°C/Gas Mark 4.

Scoop out the flesh of the zucchini and finely chop. Melt the butter in a heavy-bottom skillet and cook the zucchini flesh, stirring often, until lightly browned. Transfer to a bowl and add the feta, ricotta, gruyère, egg, marjoram, flour, salt, and pepper and mix. Fill the zucchini halves with the cheese mixture and place them side by side on a parchment (baking) paper-lined baking sheet (tray). Grill or bake for about 20 minutes, until the filling is browned and heated through. Sprinkle with parsley and serve warm.

Broccoli and Barley
with Parsley
see page 153

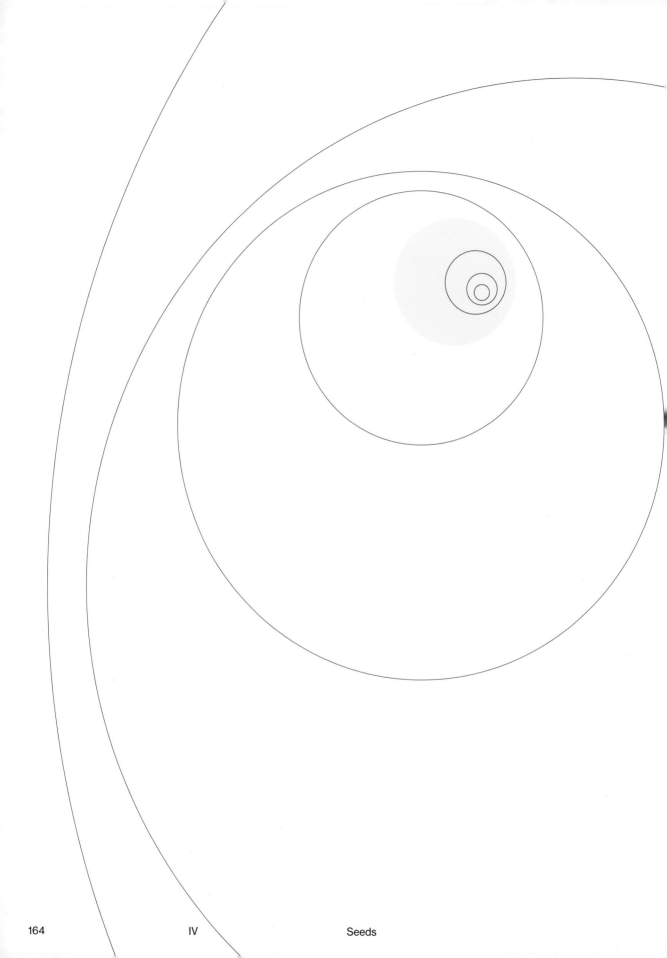

 Seeds

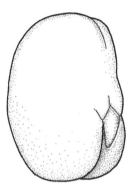

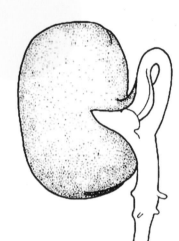

=====
Seeds

Asako Iwama and
Lauren Maurer

In our cooking, we prize the variety of seeds, the flavor and energy they provide. Whenever we can, we choose whole-grain products in our kitchen. Not only do they provide a host of minerals and fiber, they also bring vivid flavor to our dishes. As a diverse family – including grains, beans, nuts, and spices – they are among the most important sources of protein, fat, and carbohydrates in the human diet. Soybeans, lentils, rice, buckwheat, flour, cashews, hazelnuts, vanilla, cumin, and mustard are all seeds.

Seeds are small capsules of life containing an entire organism. The plant's embryo, formed after pollination, is enclosed in a nourishing coat. We plant seeds and they germinate, starting a new generation. But seeds are not only the plant's legacy. They also act as a collective memory for humans. Seeds are the promise of food, of life continuing beyond the season. This is why seeds have been carefully saved and exchanged as precious goods since the early days of agriculture. They were a currency with tangible, edible value. Early stock exchanges traded in seeds, and today, seeds have increasingly turned into a major commodity. As the global population grows, the processes of farming have been streamlined into more and more industrial-ized forms. In recent years, large corporations have developed genetically modified crops that terminate after one cycle. This disconnects agriculture from the natural cycle – from the temporal aspect of sowing, harvesting, and sowing again. Older seed varieties are pushed from the market, which affects small farmers particularly hard. Vandana Shiva's seed bank project, something we admire greatly, aims to preserve the seed heritage. For us, it is important to maintain an awareness of the potential and power of the seed, to cherish the nourishment it provides and its trajectory into the future.

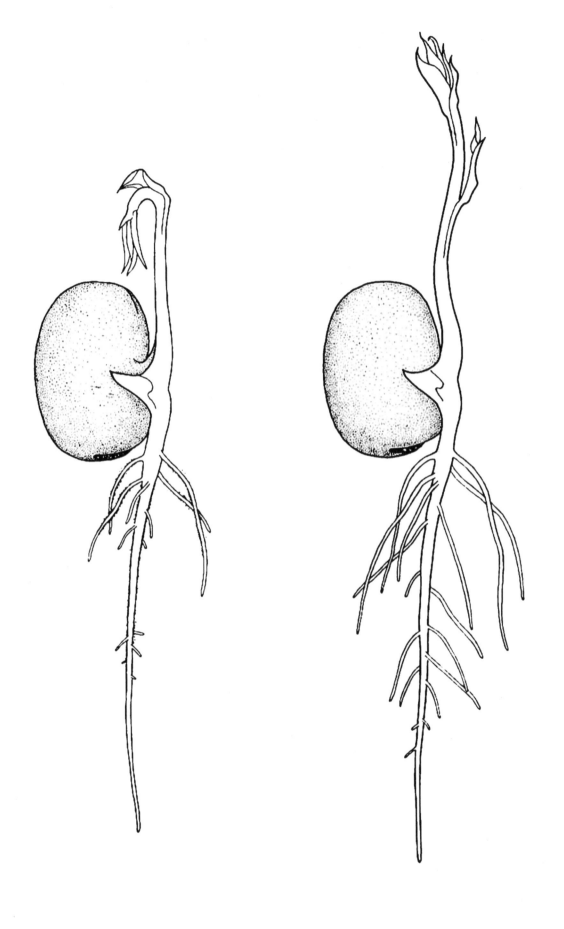

"Seeds are our most durable and concentrated foods. They're rugged lifeboats, designed to carry a plant's offspring to the shore of an uncertain future. Tease apart a whole grain, or bean, or nut, and inside you find a tiny embryonic shoot. At harvest time that shoot had entered suspended animation, ready to survive months of drought or cold while waiting for the right moment to come back to life. The bulk of the tissue that surrounds it is a food supply to nourish this rebirth. It's the distillation of the parent plant's lifework, its gathering of water and nitrogen and minerals from the soil, carbon from the air, and energy from the sun. And as such, it's an invaluable resource for us and other creatures of the animal kingdom who are unable to live on soil and sunlight and air."

Harold McGee
On Food and Cooking: The Science and Lore of the Kitchen

Anise

Valerian

Apple

Cardamom

Fennel

Pomegranate

Raspberry

Coffee

Cacao

Camomile

Cherry

Caraway

Dandelion

Maize

Mistletoe

Poppy

Nutmeg

Papaya

Sweet Pepper

Pepper

Pimiento

Castor

Rosemary

Saffron

Yarrow

Tea

Thyme

Vanilla

Walnut

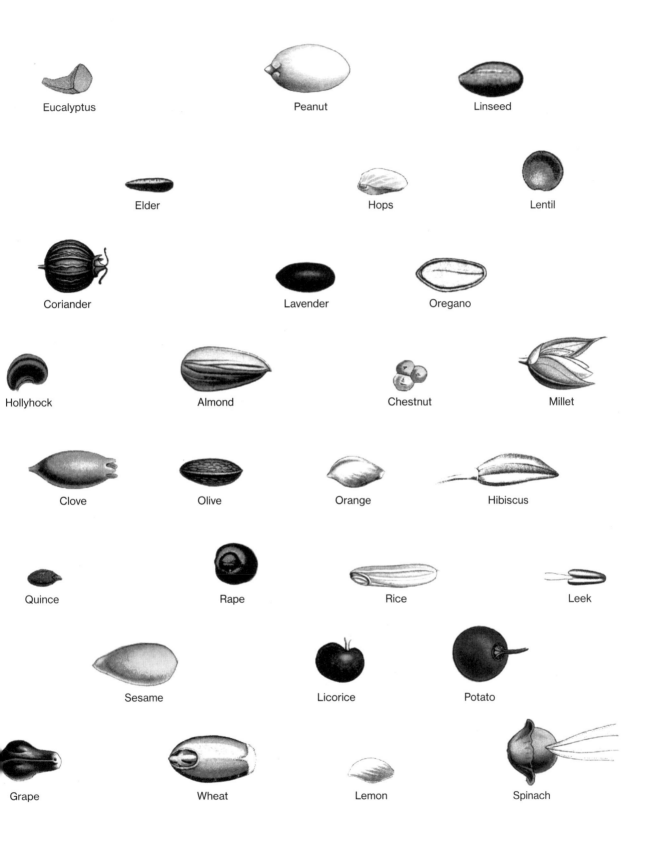

Eucalyptus

Peanut

Linseed

Elder

Hops

Lentil

Coriander

Lavender

Oregano

Hollyhock

Almond

Chestnut

Millet

Clove

Olive

Orange

Hibiscus

Quince

Rape

Rice

Leek

Sesame

Licorice

Potato

Grape

Wheat

Lemon

Spinach

"[T]he seed is as much part of the relationship with the bee and the butterfly as it is with the soil organisms that it ultimately sustains, as it is with the food that we eat. All these relationships are in the seed."

|| Vandana Shiva
The Future of Food and Seed ||

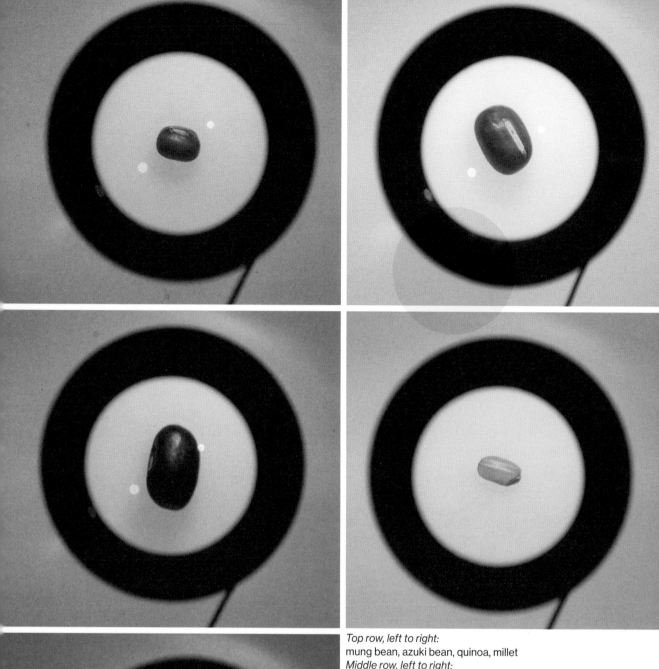

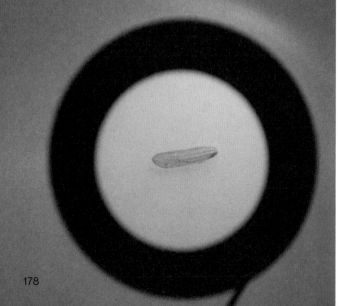

Top row, left to right:
mung bean, azuki bean, quinoa, millet
Middle row, left to right:
black bean, round grain rice, pinto bean
Bottom row, left to right:
basmati rice, mountain lentil, white bean

Seeds

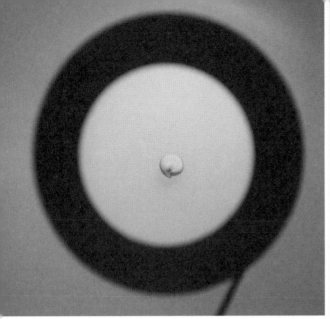

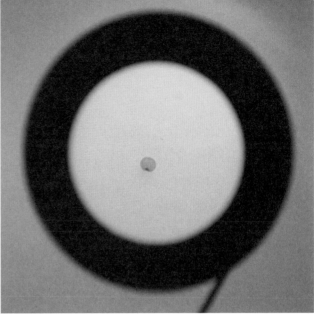

"Seed not only plays an important part in the rituals and rites of communities, it also represents the accumulation over centuries of people's knowledge and, by being a reflection of the options available to them, it represents their choice. In today's context of biological and ecological destruction, seed conservers are the true gifters of seed. Conserving seeds is conserving biodiversity. Conserving seed is thus more than merely conserving germ plasm. Conserving seed is conserving biodiversity, conserving knowledge of the seed and its utilization, conserving culture, conserving sustainability."

Vandana Shiva
Seed Dictatorship and Food Fascism

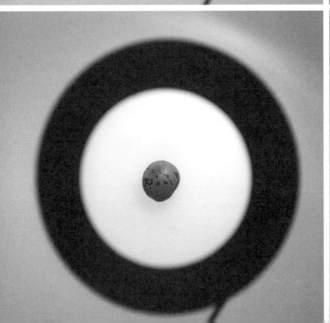

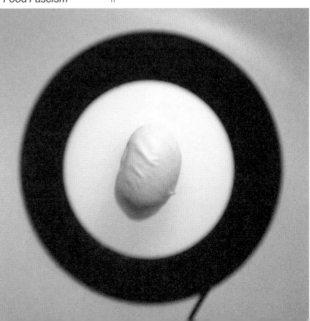

Curatorial Approach Marathon

The Curatorial Approach Marathon took place December 8–10, 2010, at the Institut für Raumexperimente. Curators from twelve art institutions around the world, participants from the institute, invited guests, and studio members joined for three days of presentations, talks, and discussions on curatorial approaches and practices. Food was eaten without "instruments," focusing on the performative and social aspects of eating. The concept "Hand as Tool, Seed as Food," conceived and performed by Asako Iwama and Lauren Maurer, additionally raised awareness and initiated thinking around seeds as an essential nutrient and legacy, a thought that shone through the choice of ingredients and dishes and was accompanied by a small leaflet created especially for the event participants.

Curatorial Approach Marathon

The hand is a delicate food utensil. Pincer and shovel and thinking peeler. "The narrowest hinge in my hand puts to scorn all machinery," wrote Walt Whitman. Hand as tool. Seeds as containers of embryonic plants, a concentrated source of protein that forms the majority of the nutrition we need. Seed as food.

Using the food as its own container: soup bowls were made of bread, the skins of the food used as wrappers. Gingerbread turned into sheets, carried as files in boxes, broken into oblique geometries. The fingers pressing the seeds into balls, sticky morsels to take for a dip.

Hands were plates, fingers silverware. *You are the dishes you use.* Washing the dishes as simple as washing the hands. Everyone did their own.

The benches we sat on to listen to talks were designed to be turned over, and became the tables we stood around to curate eating in clusters of five or six people. *You are the settings.*

A plate of foods that could be eaten with the hands, wrapped, rolled, and scooped. Beans turned into paste, grains and sauces mopped up with bread. Food made from various forms of seeds.

The meal is a small spatial dance of changing the relations of things to each other. A coordinated form of the fingers and palms inflecting to the food's form. Not the shape of the food only, but the form of being conscious of the food making the short excursion from tray to mouth to tray. Of the body as coordinated instrument of complex rhythms of repeated reaching out, touching in.

The tables being turned back over again, holding up the fed bodies, as listeners attuned to breaking down the things that were passing through them. Three packed days of content fed.

Eric Ellingsen and
Christina Werner

187

Drawing inspiration from the marathon's theme of "hand as tool; seed as food," the dishes served at the Curatorial Approach Marathon were intended to be eaten only with the hands. The absence of utensils brought focus to the ways meals can be curated, making us reflect on how we perceive ourselves tasting and eating food.

Adapted from *Jerusalem*

Falafel   Serves 6 | 60

9 oz (250 g) | 5½ lb (2.5 kg) . . .	dried chickpeas
1 | 10 cloves	garlic, crushed
1 | 10 medium	onion/s, finely chopped
1 TB | 3 bunches	fresh cilantro (coriander), chopped
¼ | 2½ tsp	cayenne pepper
¼ | 2½ tsp	ground cardamom
½ | 5 tsp	ground cumin
½ | 5 tsp	ground coriander
½ | 5 tsp	baking powder (sodium bicarbonate)
1 | 10 TB	all-purpose flour
. . . .	salt and freshly ground black pepper
3 cups (750 ml) | 7 cups (2 liters) .	olive oil for deep frying

Soak the chickpeas overnight in cold water until they have reached at least twice their original volume. Drain the chickpeas and combine them with the garlic, onion, and cilantro. Pulse the chickpea mixture in a food processor (for a large quantity, work in batches) until chopped, and then transfer to a large bowl. Mix in the spices, baking powder, flour, salt, pepper, and 3 tablespoons (2 cups/ 450 ml) water, mixing by hand until smooth. Cover and store in the refrigerator for at least 1 hour. Prepare plates or serving platters, lining them with paper towels. Pour the oil into a heavy-bottom saucepan to a depth of at least 2¾ inches (7 cm) and heat to 350°F/180°C/ Gas Mark 4. Carefully lower the purée into the hot oil one tablespoon at a time. Fry until the falafel are cooked on the inside and lightly browned on the outside, turning them with a slotted spoon when necessary. Transfer them onto the paper towels to drain. Serve immediately (or keep warm, uncovered in an oven preheated to 200°F/100°C/Gas Mark 1/2 for up to 30 minutes). Repeat the process with the remaining purée.

Hummus   Serves 6 | 60

2 | 15 cans (14 oz/400 g each) . .	chickpeas, drained
⅔ cup (150 ml) | scant 1 quart (1 liter)	tahini
⅔ cup (150 ml) | scant 1 quart (1 liter)	olive oil
1 | 8 medium	lemon/s, juiced
4 cloves | 1 head	garlic
1 pinch | 2 tsp	ground cumin
. . . .	sea salt and freshly ground black pepper

Place the chickpeas in a food processor and grind into a thick paste. With the machine still running, add the tahini, olive oil, lemon juice, garlic, cumin, and some salt. Mix for about 2 minutes until the hummus is very creamy and smooth. Season with salt and pepper to taste. Add cold water if too thick. As a variation, roasted red peppers and crushed chiles can be blended in too.

Pesto Genovese   Makes about 1 cup (240 ml)

3 large bunches	basil
1–2 cloves	garlic
. . . .	sea salt
3 TB	pine nuts or cashews
½ cup (120 ml)	extra-virgin olive oil
¼ cup (50 g)	parmesan, grated
2 or 3 TB	pecorino, grated

Gently wash and dry the basil and pick the leaves off the stems. In a food processor, first chop the garlic, salt, and pine nuts or cashews until fairly fine. Then add the basil and olive oil. When smooth, add the cheeses, and blend until combined. Season with salt to taste.

Focaccia
see page 58

Tomato Chiles Sauce
see page 114

Palak Paneer
see page 117

Sweet and Sour Dal   Serves 6 | 60

Adapted from *The Vegetarian Table: India*

7 oz (200 g)	4½ lb (2 kg) . . .	dried yellow or red lentils or yellow split peas
½	5 tsp	turmeric
1 thumb-	1 hand-sized piece . .	fresh ginger, grated
¼	2½ tsp	cayenne pepper or red chiles, crushed
1 tsp	3 TB	cumin seeds, roasted and ground
2 TB	1¼ cups (295 ml)	ghee or sunflower oil
1	8	butternut squash, peeled and cubed
⅓	3 (14 oz/400 ml) cans . . .	coconut milk
½	5 TB	mustard seeds
3 TB	7 oz (200 g)	shredded coconut
1|10	lemon/s or lime/s, zested and juiced
. . . .	salt
½	5 bunch/es	cilantro (coriander), chopped

Rinse the lentils. Drain and place in a large pot. Add scant 1 quart (1 liter) or 2⅔ gallons (10 liters) water, bring to a boil, and skim off the foam that collects on the surface. Add the turmeric, ginger, cayenne pepper, cumin, and one teaspoon of the ghee or oil. Add the squash. Turn down the heat and boil gently with the lid not completely covering the pot for 1 hour or until the lentils are very soft, stirring occasionally. Add the coconut milk and blend the soup.

About 5 minutes before serving, fry the mustard seeds in the remaining ghee or oil over medium heat. When they are slightly brown, pour the seeds and ghee into the soup and add the coconut, citrus zest and juice, and salt to taste. Bring to a gentle boil, then mix in the cilantro to finish.

Dosa   Makes about 30 dosas

Adapted from *The Vegetarian Table: India*

6¼ oz (180 g)	polenta
5 oz (140 g)	semolina
4¼ oz (120 g)	whole wheat pastry flour
2 tsp	cumin seeds
½ TB	red pepper flakes, crushed
3 TB	cilantro (coriander), chopped
1 tsp	salt
1 pinch	baking soda
. . . .	unrefined corn oil for frying, as required

Mix together the polenta, semolina, flour, cumin seeds, pepper flakes, and cilantro with 2½ cups (600 ml) water. Cover and set aside for at least 2 hours, ideally overnight. To cook the dosas, add a little more water to the polenta mixture, making a batter that is thin and pourable, and mix in the salt, soda, and ½ tablespoon of oil. Heat a nonstick skillet over medium heat. Stirring the batter between each use, pour out one ladleful into the bottom of the pan. Tilt the pan so the batter forms an 8-inch (20 cm) crêpe. When the edges begin to curl and the bottom turns golden brown, flip and cook the other side. Stack the dosas to keep them warm.

Baked and served during the Curatorial Approach Marathon, the large sheets of gingerbread were broken and shared, turning the cooking into a communal act. The unorthodox shapes and scoring of the gingerbread added an element of unpredictability to this process.

Gingerbread Cookies   Makes 15–25 small cookies or 1 large cookie

Adapted from *Breakfast, Lunch, Tea: Rose Bakery*

3 cups (370 g)	all-purpose flour
1 tsp	baking soda
½ tsp	salt
1 TB	ground dried ginger
1 TB	ground cinnamon
1	ground cardamom pod (or 1 tsp ground mixed spice)
9 TB (125 g)	butter, softened
½ cup (90 g)	brown sugar
3 TB	molasses or treacle
1–2	egg/s

Combine the flour, baking soda, salt, ground ginger, cinnamon, and cardamom in a small bowl. In a separate bowl, mix the butter with the sugar and molasses until creamy. Beat in the egg, and then fold in the dry ingredients. Add a little extra flour if the dough seems too wet. If it turns out too dry, add one more egg. Form the dough into a ball, cover with plastic wrap (cling film), and place in the refrigerator for 30 minutes.

Preheat the oven to 350°F/ 180°C/Gas Mark 4. Line a baking sheet (tray) with parchment (baking) paper. Dust your work surface with flour. Roll out the dough into a rectangle about ¼-inch (½ cm) thick, and draw long lines into the dough – not cutting through – as guides for breaking the big cookie when cooked. Alternatively, make smaller cookies with a cookie cutter. Bake for about 10 to 15 minutes until slightly firm. If cooking one big cookie, the baking time will be slightly longer.

Red Pepper and Rice Casserole Serves 6 | 60

9 oz (250 g)	5½ lb (2.5 kg) . . .	brown basmati rice
1	10	lemon/s, juiced
4 TB	3 bunches	dill, minced
. . . .	olive oil
2 medium	6 lb 11 oz (3 kg) . . .	onions, minced
5 medium	11 lb (5 kg)	red bell peppers, diced
2	20 cloves	garlic, minced
2 tsp	6 TB	dried basil
1 tsp	3 TB	dried oregano
. . . .	salt and freshly ground black pepper
5 oz (100 g)	2 lb 11 oz (1 kg) .	feta cheese, crumbled
4 oz (250 g)	5½ oz (2.5 kg) .	ricotta or cottage cheese
4	40	fresh tomatoes, sliced
3½ oz (100 g)	2 lb 4 oz (1 kg) .	kalamata olives, pitted and roughly chopped
2 TB	2 bunches	parsley, chopped

Adapted from *The New Moosewood Cookbook*

In a saucepan, cover rice with 1¾ cup (400 ml) or 3½ quarts (4 liters) water and bring to a boil. Reduce heat to low and simmer uninterrupted for about 40 minutes. When done, add the lemon juice and dill and let cool.

While the rice is cooking, heat the oil in a heavy-bottom skillet over medium heat. Gently cook the onions until golden and transfer to a large bowl. Cook the red peppers until they are tender. Add the garlic, basil, oregano, salt, and pepper. Cook for another minute or two and transfer to the bowl with the onions. Stir in the feta and ricotta.

Preheat the oven to 400°F/200°C/Gas Mark 6. Combine the rice with the onions and red peppers and mix well. Spread into an oiled casserole pan, layer tomato slices on top, and scatter the olives over the tomatoes. Bake uncovered for 30 minutes. Sprinkle with parsley and extra olive oil, and serve hot or warm with Green Salad with Balsamic Dijon Dressing (see page 353).

Beluga Lentil Salad with Cooked Fennel Serves 6 | 60

1	10	shallot/s or small onion/s, thinly sliced
1 TB	⅔ cup (150 ml)	sherry vinegar
5 oz (150 g)	3¼ lb (1.5 kg) . . .	beluga lentils
. . . .	sea salt and freshly ground black pepper
1 TB	⅔ cup (150 ml)	olive oil
1	10 medium	fennel bulb/s, quartered and thinly sliced
1 TB	⅔ cup (150 ml)	white wine (optional)
2 TB	3 bunches	flat-leaf parsley, finely chopped

Place the shallots in a bowl with the sherry vinegar and set aside.

In a pot, cover the lentils with cold water, bring to a simmer, and cook until al dente, about 15 minutes, adding water as necessary to keep the lentils just covered. Drain and add the shallots and vinegar, salt, and pepper and mix well.

While the lentils are cooking, heat the olive oil in a heavy-bottom saucepan and gently cook the fennel over medium heat for 2 minutes. Add the white wine, cover with a lid, and cook the fennel until it begins to soften. Add the fennel to the lentils, pour over the olive oil from the pan, and mix well. Sprinkle with parsley and serve.

Wakame, Sesame, and Ginger Soup   Serves 6 | 60

2 strips | 7 oz (200 g)	wakame
1 tsp | 5 TB	salt
1 TB | 5 oz (150 g)	toasted sesame seeds, roughly ground
1 thumb- | 1 hand-size piece .	ginger, finely grated
a dash | 3 TB	toasted sesame oil
. . . .	freshly ground black pepper
2 TB | 3 bunches	scallions (spring onions), finely chopped (optional)

In a large pot, soak the wakame in 6¼ cups (1.5 liters) or 5 gallons (20 liters) water for 30 minutes. Remove with a skimmer, reserving the soaking water. Cut the seaweed into 1½-inch (4 cm) pieces and set aside. Bring the water to a boil. Add salt and the sesame seeds along with the prepared wakame, ginger, sesame oil, and pepper. Add the scallions just before serving.

Brown Rice with Kimchi and Nori Flakes   Serves 6 | 60

12 oz (350 g) | 7 lb 11 oz (3.5 kg) .	brown short-grain rice
2 TB | 9 oz (250 g)	red quinoa
4 tsp | 7 oz (200 ml)	sunflower oil
7 oz (200 g) | 4½ lb (2 kg) . .	smoked tofu, cut into 1 cm cubes
. . . .	freshly ground black pepper
6 | 60	egg/s
2 tsp | 6 TB	soy sauce
7 oz (200 g) | 4½ lb (2 kg) . .	Kimchi (see page 245)
3 TB | 9 oz (250 g)	toasted sesame seeds
1 TB | 8 bunches	scallions (spring onions), finely chopped
1 | 10 sheet/s	nori, torn into small pieces

Prepare the brown rice and quinoa in the same pot, using twice as much water as rice and quinoa combined.

Heat the sunflower oil in a heavy-bottom saucepan and fry the tofu until crisp. Sprinkle with pepper and set aside. Whisk the eggs with half of the soy sauce, and then scramble over high heat. Chop the kimchi coarsely. Mix the brown rice, tofu, scrambled egg, kimchi, sesame seeds, and scallions. Sprinkle nori on top and serve with the rmaining soy sauce on the side.

Baked Chicory   Serves 6 | 60

4 medium | 6 lb 11 oz (3 kg) . . .	chicory, halved or quartered
4 tsp | scant ¾ cup (200 ml) . .	olive oil
. . . .	sea salt and freshly ground black pepper
. . . .	sherry vinegar

Place chicory, cut side up, on a baking sheet (tray) lined with parchment (baking) paper. Drizzle with the olive oil and bake for 40 minutes. Sprinkle with salt, pepper, and sherry vinegar. Vary by replacing or combining the chicory with radicchio.

Savoury Scones
see page 50

Winter White Root Soup
see page 74

Studio recipes are often inspired by a variety of sources, a diversity that this dish celebrates. Each of the ingredients has a strong and unique quality: the nutty texture of the baked beets combines nicely with the crunchiness of the onions, just as the brown rice matches well with the kale's crispness. These pairings are surprisingly intuitive, like a gentle rain that follows a billowing thundercloud.

Rain After Cloud (Beets, Kale, and Brown Rice with Crispy Onions) Serves 6 | 60

14 oz (400 g)	9 lb (4 kg) . . .	beets
. . . .	salt and freshly ground black pepper
½	5 heads	Tuscan kale, coarsely chopped
. . . .	olive oil, for drizzling
2	20	red or yellow peppers, cut into strips
4 medium	11 lb (5 kg)	onions, thinly sliced
a pinch	all-purpose flour
1 cup (250 ml)	1 quart (1 liter) . .	sunflower oil for frying
12 oz (350 g)	7 lb 12 oz (3.5 kg) .	short-grain brown or white rice (for cooking method, see page 314)
2 TB	1¼ cup (300 ml)	balsamic vinegar

Preheat the oven to 425°F/220°C/Gas Mark 7. Place the unpeeled beets on a baking sheet (tray), cover with foil, and bake for 50 minutes, until tender. When cool enough to handle, peel and slice beets as you would apples.

Pour olive oil liberally over the kale and season with salt and pepper. Spread on a baking sheet and bake for 30 minutes, until crunchy. Remove the kale from the oven and reduce the temperature to 350°F/180°C/Gas Mark 4. Toss the peppers in olive oil, salt, and pepper. Then spread on a separate baking sheet and bake for 30 minutes.

Place the onions on a large flat plate, sprinkle with flour and 1 teaspoon salt, and mix well with your hands. Heat the sunflower oil in a heavy-bottom saucepan over high heat. Test to make sure that the oil is hot: if you throw in a small piece of onion, it should sizzle vigorously. Reduce the heat to medium and carefully add one third of the sliced onions. Fry for 5 to 7 minutes, stirring occasionally, until the onions turn golden and crispy. Using a slotted spoon, transfer the onions to a colander lined with paper towels and season with a little more salt while they drain. Repeat twice more with remaining onions, adding a little more oil to the pan as needed.

Combine the cooked rice, beets, and baked peppers with the balsamic vinegar. Serve in bowls topped with the baked kale chips and crunchy onions. Serve with Salsa Verde (see page 58).

Roasted Squash and Lentil Salad Serves 6 | 60

1	8 medium	red kuri squash, seeded and cubed
3½ TB	2 cups (500 ml)	olive oil
a few sprigs	1 bunch	fresh thyme, finely chopped
½	5	small dried red chiles, crushed
. . . .	sea salt and freshly ground black pepper
1	10	shallot/s, thinly sliced
4 TB	2½ cups (600 ml)	balsamic vinegar
7 oz (200 g)	4½ lb (2 kg) . . .	puy lentils
2 TB	9 oz (250 g)	roasted squash seeds (optional)
a few sprigs	1 bunch	flat-leaf parsley, chopped
1¾ oz (50 g)	1 lb 2 oz (500 g) .	feta (optional)

Preheat the oven to 425°F/220°C/Gas Mark 7. Marinate the squash in some of the olive oil with thyme, chiles, salt, and pepper. Spread on a baking sheet (tray) and roast for 25 minutes or until easily pierced with a fork.

Place the shallots in a bowl with the balsamic vinegar and set aside.

In a pot, cover the lentils with cold water and bring to a simmer. Cook until al dente, about 20 minutes, adding water as necessary to keep the lentils just covered. Drain and combine with the shallots; season with salt and pepper to taste. Add the remaining olive oil, roasted squash, and squash seeds, and gently fold into the lentils. Sprinkle with parsley and feta and serve.

Kısır   Serves 6 | 60

By Aykan Safoğlu, former member of the kitchen team

1¾ oz (50 g)	11 lb (5 kg)	fine bulgur wheat
2 tsp	6 TB	Biber Salçası (see below)
. . . .	sea salt and freshly ground black pepper
1	10	lemon/s, juiced
5 stems	5 bunches	scallions (spring onions), finely chopped
1	7 bunch/es	flat-leaf parsley, finely chopped
¼ cup (50 ml)	generous 2 cups (500 ml) . .	olive oil
1 tsp	3–4 TB	ground cumin
1 tsp	3 TB	Turkish sumac
1	8 small	red dried chile/s
½	5 tsp	black peppercorns

Place the bulgur in a fine strainer (sieve) and rinse under cold water until the water runs clear and most of the starch has been removed. If you can't get fine bulgur, or if the package doesn't mention the grade, pour equal amounts boiling water and bulgur into a bowl and let soak for 5 minutes with a closed lid.

Transfer the bulgur to a large mixing bowl. Thin the pepper paste with a bit of water and pour over the bulgur, adding salt and pepper. Mix with your hands. Don't be afraid to massage the grains! Add lemon juice, scallions, parsley, and olive oil and mix again. Add the cumin and sumac spice, and then mix and add salt and pepper if necessary. In a mortar, grind the chiles with peppercorns and add to the bulgur as desired. When the mixture is pungently tart, spicy, and salty with hints of the greens, the Kısır is ready to serve.

Biber Salçası (Red Pepper Paste)

By Aykan Safoğlu

6 lb 11 oz (3 kg)	long red peppers, halved and seeded
. . . .	salt
. . . .	vinegar (optional)
. . . .	hot red chiles (optional)

Preheat oven to 425°F / 220°C / Gas Mark 7. Place the peppers in the oven and bake until charred. When they are cool enough to handle, peel them, and blend in a food processor.

Place the mixture in a heavy-bottom pan and bring to a boil. Lower the heat and simmer for about 25 minutes. Stir constantly. Add salt and a bit of vinegar and chiles, if you like, and mix well. Let cool.

Pinto Beans with Kohlrabi, Radishes, and Fresh Cilantro   Serves 6 | 60

5 oz (150 g)	3¼ lb (1.5 kg) . . .	pinto beans, soaked overnight
3 TB	2 cups (450 ml)	olive oil, plus extra for drizzling
11 oz (300 g)	6 lb 11 oz (3 kg) . .	mixed radishes (such as navet, daikon, or round red), peeled and diced
½	5	kohlrabi, peeled and diced
3 TB	2 cups (450 ml)	white wine
1	8	lemon/s, juiced and zested
1	10 clove/s	garlic, crushed
a few sprigs	2 bunches	cilantro (coriander), roughly chopped
2 TB	11 oz (300 g)	sesame seeds, toasted
. . . .	salt and freshly ground black pepper

In a pot, cover the beans with cold water and cook until tender – you should be able to squish them between your fingers – about 60 to 80 minutes. Add water as necessary to keep the beans just covered. Drain well when done. While the beans are cooking, heat the olive oil in a heavy-bottom saucepan, add the radishes and kohlrabi, and gently cook over medium heat for a few minutes. Add the white wine, cover, and cook until the vegetables soften. Mix with the beans and add lemon juice and zest, garlic, cilantro, sesame seeds, salt, and pepper. Drizzle with olive oil, mix well, and serve.

Baked Chicory
see page 196

Bifun Rice Noodle Salad with Peanut Sauce — Serves 6 | 60

For the salad

2 | 20 TB	sesame seeds, toasted
2 | 20	eggs
2 tsp | 6 TB	shoyu soy sauce
. . . .	freshly ground black pepper
2 TB | 1 1/4 cup (300 ml) . . .	sunflower oil
7 oz (200 g) | 4½ lb (2 kg) . . .	smoked tofu, sliced
7 oz (200 g) | 4½ lb (2 kg) . . .	mixed mushrooms (shiitake, oyster, king trumpet), sliced
. . . .	salt
9 oz (250 g) | 5½ lb (2.5 kg) . .	rice or glass noodles
4 TB | 2½ cups (600 ml)	toasted sesame oil
1 | 10	cucumber or zucchini, cut into matchsticks
1 | 10	red bell pepper/s, finely sliced
1 | 10	celery stick/s, finely sliced
10 | 4½ lb (2 kg)	cherry tomatoes, quartered
2 TB | 1 lb 2 oz (500 g)	cashews, toasted
1 | 10 bunch/es	cilantro (coriander) or basil, chopped
1 sprig | 1 bunch	mint leaves, chopped

For the peanut sauce

4 TB | 1¾ lb (800 g)	smooth peanut butter
2 TB | 1¼ cup (300 ml)	tahini
1 TB | 5 oz (150 g)	brown sugar
1½ TB | 1 scant cup (225 ml) . .	soy sauce, plus more as needed
1 tsp | 3 TB	ground chiles
50 | 1 lb 2 oz (500 g)	toasted peanuts

Toast the sesame seeds in a dry frying pan over low heat until the seeds take on a round shape. Once the pan gets hot, the seeds burn very easily, so watch out! This can be done in a large batch ahead of time and stored in a dry place for later use.

Whisk the eggs with soy sauce and pepper and scramble them in a bit of sunflower oil. Using the same frying pan, add more sunflower oil and fry the tofu until crunchy. Season with pepper and set aside. Cook the mushrooms in the pan with the soy sauce until all liquid has evaporated.

Bring a large saucepan of water to a boil and add a dash of salt. Turn off the heat, place the noodles in the water and leave for 1 minute. Drain very well and drizzle with sesame oil. Add the cucumber, red pepper, celery, sesame seeds, tomatoes, cashews, eggs, tofu, cilantro, and mint and gently mix.

For the peanut sauce, combine all ingredients. Thin with water until you reach desired consistency. Serve with the salad.

Baked Eggplant — Serves 6 | 60

1 medium | 11 lb (5 kg)	eggplant/s (aubergine/s)
. . . .	sea salt
1 TB | ⅔ cup (150 ml)	toasted sesame oil
1 tsp | 3 TB	fresh ginger, grated
2 TB | 7 oz (200 g)	sesame seeds, toasted
. . . .	Caramelized Soy Sauce (see below)

Cut the eggplants into ½-inch (1 cm) thick slices. Sprinkle with salt and set aside for 1 hour to release the bitter juices. Rinse with cold water, drain, and pat dry with a paper towel. Place in a large bowl and marinate in the sesame oil.

Preheat the oven to 400°F/ 200°C/Gas Mark 7. Place the eggplant on a baking sheet (tray) lined with parchment (baking) paper. Bake for 20 minutes, turn the slices over, and bake for another 15 minutes. To serve, sprinkle the eggplant with ginger, sesame seeds, and Caramelized Soy Sauce.

Caramelized Soy Sauce — Makes 1⅔ cups (400 ml)

scant ½ cup (100 ml)	sesame or peanut oil
3 cloves	garlic, chopped
1 thumb-size piece	fresh ginger, grated
2	scallions (spring onions), finely chopped
3 small	dried red chiles
generous ¾ cup (200 ml) . . .	soy sauce
3 TB	brown sugar

Combine the oil, garlic, ginger, scallions, and chiles in a heavy-bottom saucepan and heat slowly until the flavors begin to meld. Add the soy sauce, brown sugar, and scant ½ cup (100 ml) water, and simmer until the mixture caramelizes slightly.

(If using the sauce with our Baked Eggplant [see above], this recipe will serve at least 60. The sauce can also be made ahead of time, and any extra can be refrigerated.)

We try very hard to keep the kitchen as seasonal as possible. Because of this, from late fall to early spring, we cook with a lot of pumpkin, squash, and root vegetables. During the winter, we prepare white salads instead of green ones because of all the radishes, celery, and fennel that are in season.

Winter Squash, Chestnut, and Barley Soup   Serves 6 | 60

Adapted from *River Cafe Cook Book Two*

5 oz (150 g)	3¼ lb (1.5 kg) . . .	barley
1	22 lb (10 kg)	red kuri squash, seeded and chopped
scant ½ cup (100 ml)	1 quart (1 liter)	olive oil
2 cloves	1 head	garlic, minced
a few sprigs	6 bunches . . .	rosemary, chopped
a pinch	1 tsp	small dried red chiles, crushed
. . . .	sea salt and freshly ground black pepper
3½ oz (100 g)	2 lb 11 oz (1 kg) .	chestnuts
3 medium	6 lb 11 oz (3 kg) . . .	onions, finely chopped
1	8 head/s	celery, chopped
¼ cup (50 ml)	generous 2 cups (500 ml) . .	white wine
6¼ cups (1.5 liters)	4 gallons (15 liters)	Vegetable Stock (see page 74) or water

Preheat the oven to 400°F/200°C/Gas Mark 6. Soak the barley in cold water for 30 minutes. While the barley is soaking, marinate the squash in some of the oil, half of the garlic, rosemary, and chiles, as well as salt and pepper, and spread onto a baking sheet (tray). Bake for 40 minutes.

In the same water it has been soaking in, boil the barley for about 30 minutes, or until al dente; set aside. Prepare the chestnuts by cutting their skins crosswise. Roast them on a baking sheet for about 30 minutes. Let them sit until cool enough to handle before peeling and chopping them coarsely. (Alternatively, use packed, precooked chestnuts.)

Heat the oil in a large, heavy-bottom saucepan and gently cook the onions with celery and the remaining garlic, rosemary, and chiles until lightly browned. Add the white wine and simmer for 10 minutes. Add the vegetable stock or water and bring to a boil. Add the roasted squash, chopped chestnuts, and cooked barley and bring to a boil. Season with salt and pepper, drizzle with olive oil, and serve.

Mung Bean and Dill Salad   Serves 6 | 60

5 oz (150 g)	3¼ lb (1.5 kg) . . .	mung beans
1	8	lemons, juiced and zested
1	8 tsp	ume su (see page 241)
1	10 clove/s	garlic, crushed
2¼ oz (60 g)	1 lb 5 oz (600 g) .	sun-dried tomatoes in oil, chopped, oil reserved
1	6 bunches	dill, finely chopped
4 medium	5 kg	zucchini, very thinly sliced
2 TB	250 g	sunflower seeds, toasted
. . . .	salt and freshly ground black pepper

In a pot, cover the mung beans with cold water, bring to a simmer, and cook until al dente, about 15 minutes, adding water as necessary to keep the beans just covered. Drain well when done. Mix in the lemon juice, zest, ume su, garlic, and tomatoes with their oil. Add the dill, zucchini, and sunflower seeds, and toss to combine. Season to taste with salt and pepper.

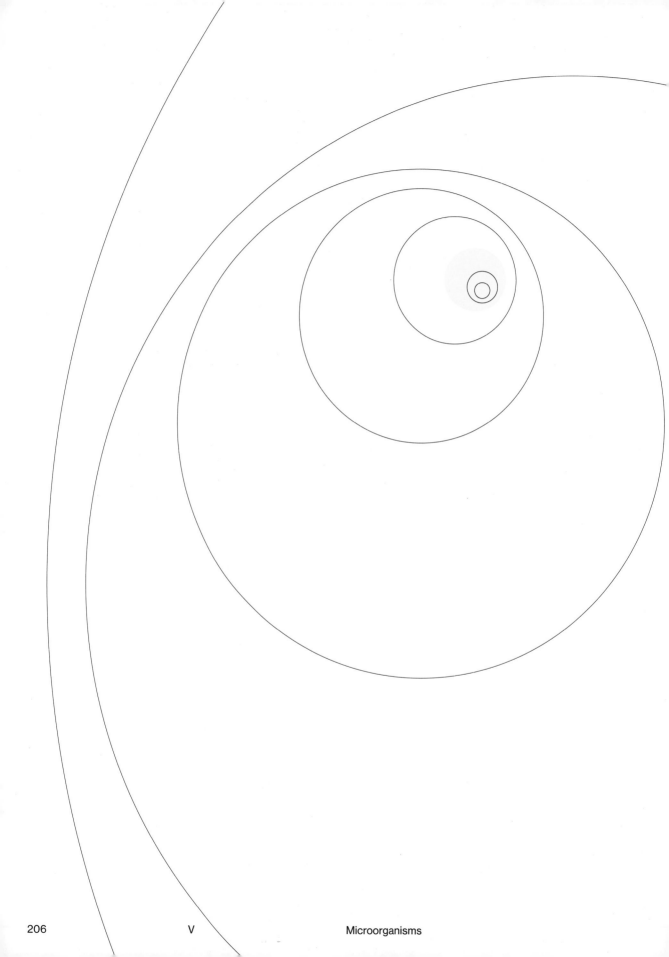

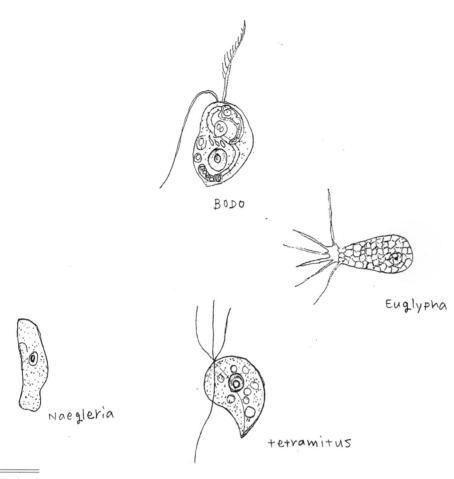

BODO

Euglypha

Naegleria

tetramitus

Microorganisms

Asako Iwama and
Lauren Maurer

While some bacteria are harmful, most are beneficial to human life. In our bodies, we carry approximately two to five pounds (one to two kilograms) of gut bacteria. These microorganisms aid the digestion of food and fuel our metabolism. Their balanced interplay helps us work. It is a fully functioning energy cycle: we eat, digest, are energized, live, and create.

In our gardening and cooking, bacteria feature in different ways. We have practiced composting for some years, using a custom-built rotating composter for trimmed parts of fruit and vegetables or coffee grounds from the kitchen. With the help of bacteria, these are turned into fertile soil, which we transfer back into the cycle of organic growth by using it in our roof garden and the planters in front of the studio. Microorganisms also play a substantial role in how we prepare and preserve food: pickles are created by blocking the microbial processes, and microorganisms are the agents of fermentation. Worldwide, up to one third of foods are fermented — among them such staples as leavened bread and yogurt. Fermentation adds flavor, and it makes some foods easier to digest or more nutritious.

Waiting for dough to rise, for the taste of pickled vegetables to develop, or for the flavor of miso or kimchi to reach the desired intensity requires time. It cannot be rushed. Its temporal trajectory slows us down. For us, the act of waiting is an opportunity: it opens the door to a more conscious rootedness in the now. It creates awareness of time and the process of becoming.

Bacteria were the first life forms on our planet. They are known as prokaryote and consist of a single nucleus with no enclosing membrane. Their main purpose is to replicate. In the early stages of evolution, they were the agents that turned inorganic matter into fertile soil. Eventually, a green carpet of plants covered Earth. Through photosynthesis, this carpet produced oxygen, creating a habitat for other living organisms.

Today, it may seem as if humans have harnessed bacteria. Yet the truth remains that far from mastering microbial processes, humans are a result of them. Taking a closer look at bacteria challenges many preconceptions. It ultimately questions the dominating anthropocentric perspective today.

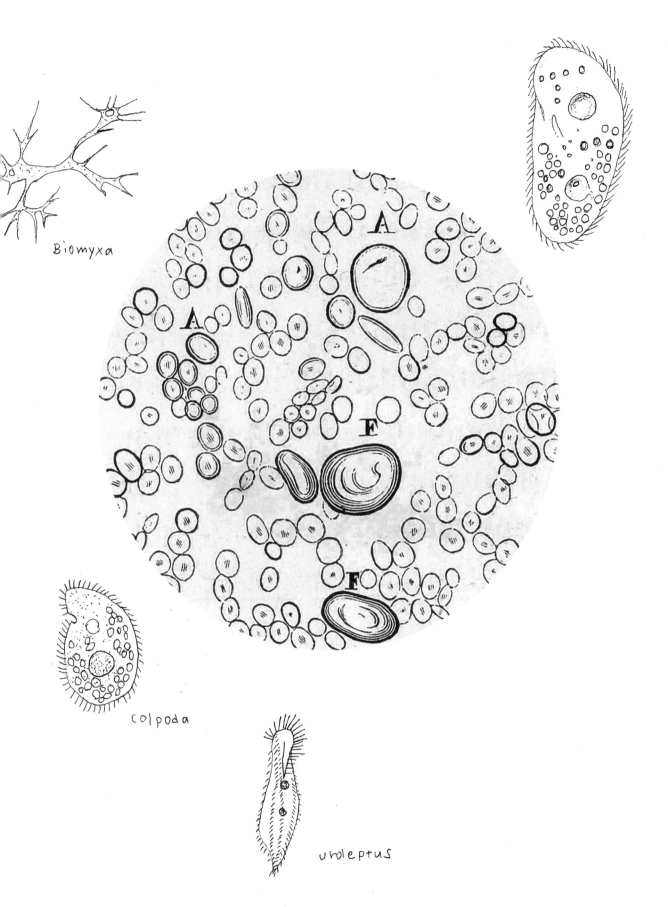

Biomyxa

colpoda

uroleptus

 Microorganisms

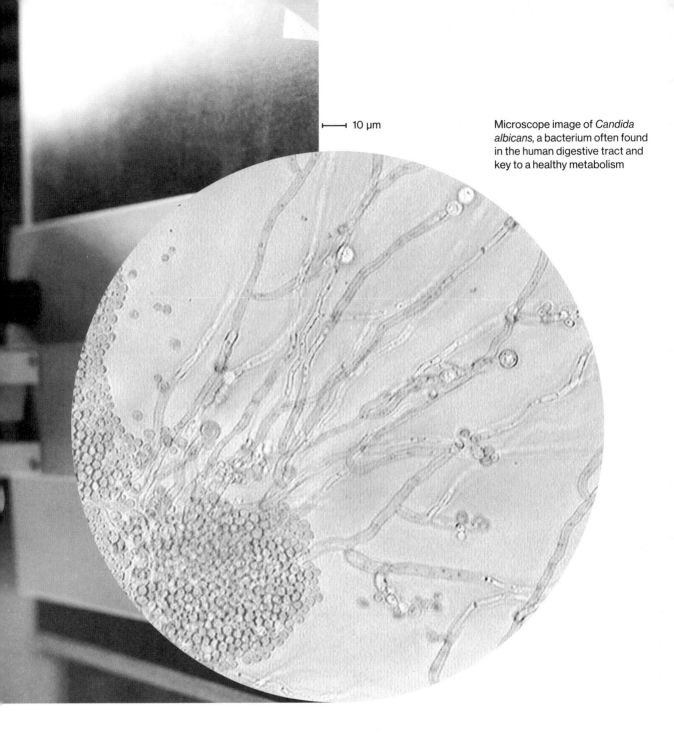

├──────┤ 10 μm

Microscope image of *Candida
albicans,* a bacterium often found
in the human digestive tract and
key to a healthy metabolism

Left: Mushrooms grown in the studio kitchen (*Pleurotus eryngii*)

Top: Microscope image of *Aspergillus* mold, central to many fermentation processes

Bottom: Illustration of various microorganisms

40 μm

"The process of recycling returns materials to a previous stage in a repetitive process. In a natural ecosystem, the wastes from one process become the resources for other processes . . .

In other words, there is no waste in nature, but a continuous flow of materials and energy from one organism to another through basic cycles such as the carbon, nitrogen, or water cycle. Our current industrial society treats waste as something to throw away, to get rid of, to dispose of. We need to change the way we think about waste. We need to think, 'Waste is a resource. Resources have value.' And we need to ask ourselves, 'How can we move from a wasteful society to a waste-free society?' Worm bins could contribute significantly to achieving the goal of a waste-free or zero-waste society. Food residues turn into plant nutrients through the action of worms."

|| Mary Appelhof ||
|| *Worms Eat My Garbage* ||

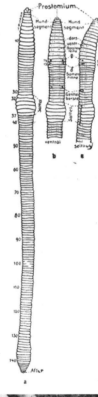

かぼちゃの ツル が 屋根 からのびてくる

· Cooking - functional activities

· something that makes people think of certain things

· taste them at the moment they let go of the soil, you learn to respect them.

かぼちゃ

菌類による植物の病気：月の力が地球にあまりに強く影響したとき、菌類は、自分の本来の居場所である地表を去るのだ.

スギナ : Equisetum arvense

料理 は文献になったのはいつ？

料理の技術はどうやって伝わったのか!?

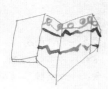

年表 / マットロッグ

おりこみ

チャプターのぶ分け

目で見て一度にわかる.

○ 医学としての食　マクロビオティック

○ 自給自足

○ 種

○ 農業という技術　継承していくという事

= 絶滅する生物・植物

○ 微生物：土壌は彼らが初めて作り出したのである。
バクテリア　歯も口もたない彼らは、地球という名で呼ばれる
microorganism 以前に彼らが相続した一惑星の
味つけされた元素を 個膜を通して摂取し、
化学作用によって咀嚼し、死骸となって腐植質という生きた土壌を
作り出した。

土壌の神秘
P.81

To projection of microorganism

bacterium

細菌

ハチミツ
ハワイ
www.volcanoislandhoney.com

The biology and population dynamics of social insects and their pests, parasites and pathogens

- Dr. Stephen J. Martin ● Uni of Sheffield

"Every living creature on this Earth interacts intimately with its environment via its food. Humans in our developed technological society, however, have largely severed this connection, and with disastrous results. Though affluent people have more food choices than people of the past could ever have dreamed of, and though one person's labor can produce more food today than ever before, the large-scale, commercial methods and systems that enable these phenomena are destroying our Earth, destroying our health, and depriving us of dignity. With respect to food, the vast majority of people are completely dependent for survival upon a fragile global infrastructure of monocultures, synthetic chemicals, biotechnology, and transportation.

Moving toward a more harmonious way of life and greater resilience requires our active participation. This means finding ways to become more aware of and connected to the other forms of life that are around us and that constitute our food – plants and animals, as well as bacteria and fungi – and to the resources, such as water, fuel, materials, tools, and transportation, upon which we depend. It means taking responsibility for our shit, both literally and figuratively."

‖ Sandor Ellix Katz ‖
The Art of Fermentation

* Quoted from Matsuo Bashō's
"Notes from a Walk in the Wild".
Two lines reference the poem
"Travel in the Morning" by Du Mu,
a Chinese poet from the Tang
Dynasty: "I put down the whip
and let the horse walk / for miles
no cock crowing is heard. /
To carry on the unfinished dream
in a forest / Suddenly scared
by fallen leaves."

Untitled (To Miso That Arrived Late) Hu Fang, poet

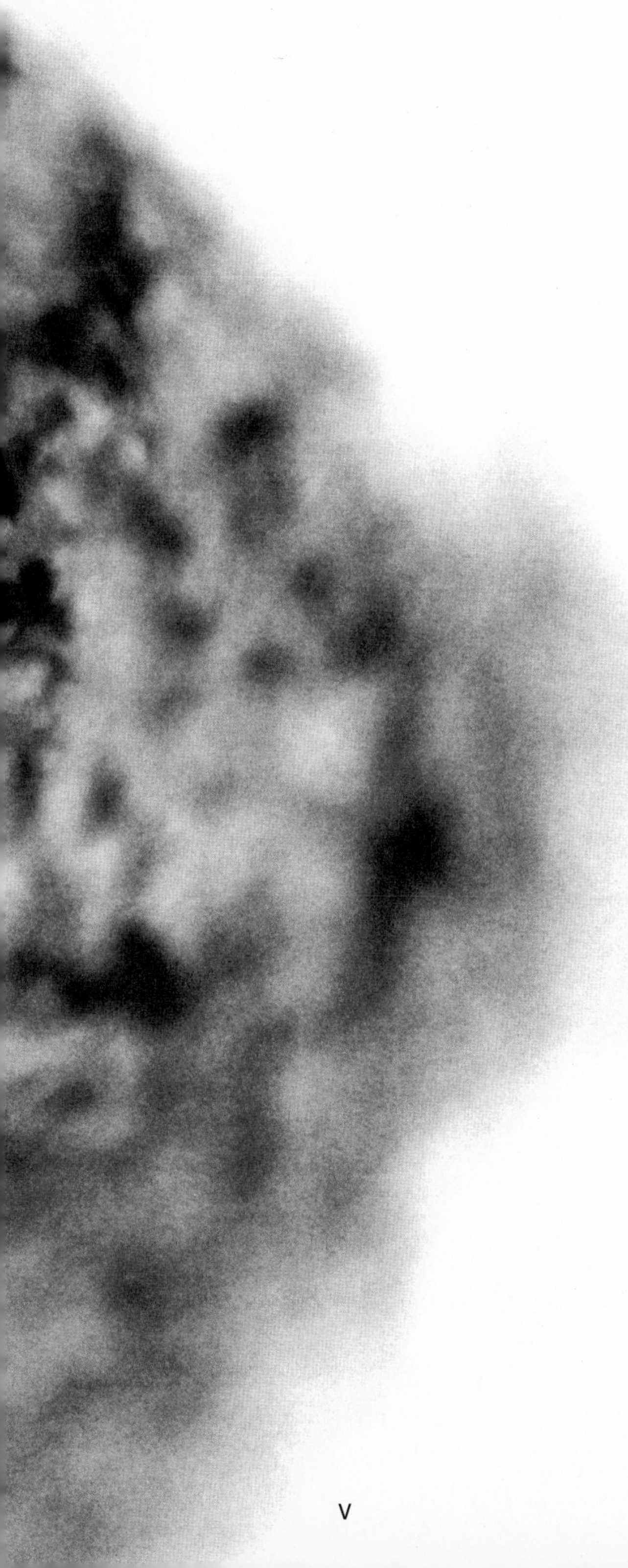

The miso you
promised to make for me,
I have not yet received it.

A room in preparation of a journey.
A kitchen after a farewell.
All left in a mess.

Those distant places, indescribable and yet to be proved,
always seem to be expecting something.
A meteor.
A seed that adapts to all changes.
A troubled heart.

Your writings are
drowned out by waves of wheat grains,
the secret recipe that will fulfill your wish is
lost in South China.
The black-haired girl who is obsessed with fragments
of ancient porcelain once picked them up one by one,
formed recognizable
sentences.

This, one
That, two
And then, three drops of koji
four beans
five grains of rice
six grains of salt
(distilled from seawater collected from around the Himalayas)
seven moods of waiting
(steamed from the rivers and seas within our bodies)
— all are given to the mysterious kitchen of time.

From the face of time to its end.
A reckless traveler.
The beans dedicate themselves to
fermenting a pathway,
like a shortcut from the hollow of one's hand to its back.
Only in midst of turning.
Only in midst of thirst.
She arrived,
though so very late.
Arose in me the depths of the mountain of night,
with her taste.
Awakening from a dream on the back of a horse,
the moon is far away, steam rises from hot tea. *

The ocean from the old past hides inside our bodies,
while I continue to wait.
Those breathless seeds,
moving in the speed of light within,
collapse into black holes.
The bacteria, secretly, in the darkness of night,
will eventually create
a taste
that embraces our reunion.

After preparing the miso in the summer of 2012, the kitchen team left it to ferment for more than a year down in the cold dark of the basement. Thórdís was particularly excited by the idea that it wasn't merely a recipe but rather a living thing. Every two to three months, the kitchen team visited the miso and observed it as it slowly transformed.

Miso Makes 3¼ lb (1.5 kg)

1 lb 5 oz (600 g)	soybeans
1 lb 5 oz (600 g)	rice koji (dried)*
7 oz (200 g)	salt

Wash the soybeans and put them in a bowl with four times as much cold water as soybeans. Soak the beans for 8 hours in the summer and 14 hours in the winter.

Put the soybeans and water into a saucepan and bring to a boil. When the water boils, reduce the heat to low and simmer, covered, for about 4 to 5 hours until the beans are very tender and easy to squish between fingers. During the cooking process, add water as necessary to keep the beans just covered. Stir often to keep the beans from burning or sticking to the bottom of the pot. When the beans are done, remove from heat, and let them sit overnight in the water.

On the following day, in a separate bowl, mix the dried koji and salt together using your fingers. (It is important that the koji and salt are completely combined.) Over medium heat, bring the beans to a boil and then remove from heat. Take the beans out a little at a time with a slotted spoon, and grind with a mortar and pestle, hand mixer, or food processor. The beans should be ground while hot for a smoother consistency. They should become starchy, and it's fine if the paste is not completely smooth.

Mix the bean paste and the koji with your hands into 6-inch (15 cm) balls. They should be firm, with no air inside. Throw the balls forcefully into a storing container to help release any trapped air. Punch down the balls to make sure there is no air inside. Continue this process until all miso paste is in the container. Flatten the paste and cover with a ¼-inch (5 mm) layer of salt. Cover with plastic wrap and place a 2¼ pound (1 kg) weight on top. Cover with a cloth to keep completely dust-free.

Store in a dark, cool place for 6 months. (The miso is delicious when served with fresh vegetable sticks or used in soups and various other recipes.)

* Koji is a fungus or mold called *Aspergillus oryzae*. It can be made at home or purchased.

Members of the workshop
baking pizza, Pfefferberg, 2012

When the kitchen staff consisted only of two, impromptu help was sometimes needed from the workshop team if either Asako or Lauren was absent. On one occasion, when both were away, the decision was made to make pizza. The members of the metal workshop improvised an attachment for their drill press to mix the dough, using the morning to cook up a different kind of artwork.

Pizza Dough	Makes six 10-inch (25 cm) pizzas

Adapted from *The River Cafe Cook Book Two*

4 tsp	dried yeast
1 lb 2 oz (500 g)	all-purpose flour, plus extra for dusting
5 oz (150 g)	rye flour
2 TB	milk
4 TB	olive oil
1 TB	sea salt

In a large bowl, mix the yeast with ½ cup (125 ml) warm water. When it has dissolved, let it stand 10 minutes to activate. Then add flours, milk, oil, salt, and 1 cup (250 ml) water, and stir well to combine. Knead the dough for 10 to 15 minutes. The dough will be quite wet and sticky. Return the dough to a bowl greased with olive oil. Drizzle a little oil over the top of the dough. Cover with a slightly damp cloth and leave to rise in a warm place for 2 hours.

Punch the dough down and knead again a few times; then return it to the bowl and leave to rise again for 30 minutes.

Preheat the oven to 450°F/230°C/Gas Mark 8. When the dough has risen a second time, divide it into six equal pieces and form into balls. On a well-floured surface, press out each ball as thinly as possible. Place on a baking sheet (tray), top as desired, and bake until crisp.

Christine's original recipe for this bread, passed on to her by a Swiss friend, included a peculiar step: knead the dough until doing so produces a certain belching sound. The recipe included a telephone number and instructed her to call the friend for consultation if the dough failed to emit the right noise. Christine's copy now has three telephone numbers crossed out and a fourth written in – a testimony of their long, ongoing friendship.

Braided Bread   Makes one loaf

By Christine Bopp, member of the kitchen team

1¼ oz (30 g)	fresh yeast, crumbled
1 tsp	sugar
generous 2 cups (500 ml)	milk
12 TB (170 g)	butter
2¼ lb (1 kg)	all-purpose flour, plus extra for dusting
1 TB	sea salt
1	egg, whisked
1	egg yolk, for egg wash

In a large mixing bowl, combine the yeast, sugar, and half of the milk. In a pan over low heat, melt the butter with the remainder of the milk, making sure that the mixture does not become hot or boil. Pour the warm butter and milk mixture into the yeast mixture, add the flour, salt, and egg, and knead into a dough. Cover the bowl with a warm, damp cloth, and let sit, undisturbed, until the dough has risen and doubled, about 1 hour.

Preheat the oven to 350°F/180°C/Gas Mark 4. When the dough has risen, turn it onto a floured surface and divide in half. Roll out each half into a 24-inch (60 cm) long strand, place one strand on top of the other in the shape of an *X*, and braid together.

Brush the egg wash over the dough and bake on a baking sheet (tray) on the middle rack for 45 minutes, until golden brown.

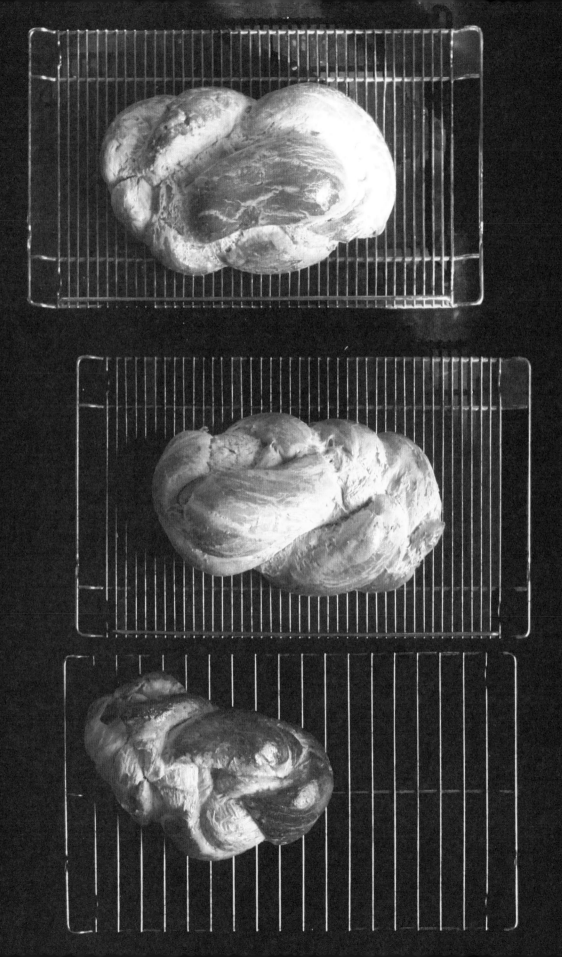

Grey sheep, native to Iceland, were long unpopular because their coloring made them difficult to find in the rocky landscape. Olafur Eliasson has been breeding grey sheep in Iceland since 2010.

Grey Sheep is also the name of a small project space that is tucked away in a corner of the Pfefferberg complex, next to Studio Olafur Eliasson. Curated by Caroline Eggel, the program is dedicated to encouraging dialog between a local audience and artists associated with the studio or the Institut für Raumexperimente.

Grey Sheep

The space we call Grey Sheep is spatially unassuming, yet it is a space of possibility, a space not born but emerging. It is a shared and collective space, not simply limited to the small room on the ground floor of the studio outside the main building. Its identity is transmitted when it is visited. You talk about it. What develops and comes to life here is dependent upon everything surrounding it and connected to it. Grey Sheep's mode is one of reaching out, of exuberance. It grows through its generosity, its gesture of hospitality: we communicate projects by word of mouth, visit them in passing, are sometimes lured by their scent. We want a taste of what

we're smelling. The garden, the produce, cooking, eating, digesting: a cycle of constant renewal and displacement.

In spring 2010, we launched the Grey Sheep project with small table installations from 1972 by Peter Weibel. Many exhibitions have followed since then: reflections through a window across the courtyard (Ivana Franke). A flashlight shines on us and follows us with its cone of light (Euan Williams). A bolt of lightning takes us by surprise! A rotating light bulb slowly probes the quality of our sight (Wolfgang Breuer). And then color appears (Jesper Dyrehauge and Alvaro Urbano).

A flag on the roof flaps in the breeze (Raul Walch). Poetry, inspired by the richness of the Pfefferberg location, is broadcast to the visitors and into the streets beyond (Kirsten Palz). We run confidently, warming ourselves in the process (Mihret Kebede). Pfefferberg brews beer again, reviving its former function as a brewery (Anders Hellsten Nissen). A whisper and the smell of malt or dill. A drop for the mind and a bite for the mood, always moving.

Caroline Eggel, head of exhibitions and production at Studio Olafur Eliasson

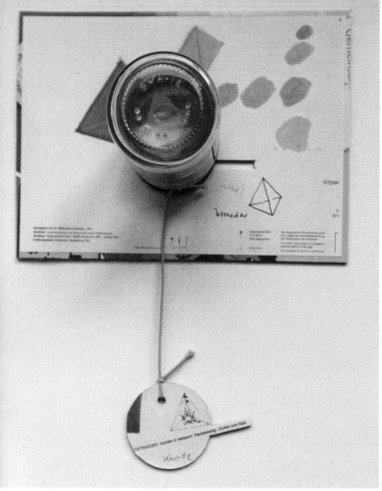

Grey Sheep

On July 20, 2011, studio members, guests, and students from the Institut für Raumexperimente gathered in the open courtyard of Pfefferberg for an opening at Grey Sheep. For the group exhibition, seasonal vegetables from the rooftop garden – harvested, fermented, and pickled by Asako Iwama, Lauren Maurer, and Clara Jo – were served from a mobile kitchen developed by Raul Walch. Leon Eixenberger's flavored marzipan cubes questioned general assumptions about taste, shape, and color, and Jeremias Holliger combined drawings with root vegetables that he had cut into geometrical shapes and pickled – playful, tasty indicators of biodynamic knowledge and cultivated forms of food and health traditions. Floating walls conceived by Quynh Vantu gently eased visitors down a sloped passage and up again, offering a detour much in the spirit of the walks often conducted by the institute. Cutlery extensions, also created by Vantu, fostered communication and inspired new table manners. In this way, the exhibition brought together the experiences of sharing food and of navigating space with traditional forms of food preservation, preserving not only flavors but also time.

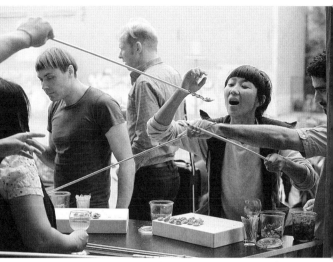

When we were planning the menu for the July 2011 Grey Sheep event, we needed something crunchy to complement the Fresh Garden Pickles (see page 237) and something salty to match the Puréed Apricot (below). We tested quite a few recipes before settling on this one, inspired by a Japanese recipe that Asako found.

Crackers   Makes about 35 crackers

Adapted from *Honkide oyatsu* (Serious Snacks)

3½ TB (50 g)	ghee or butter, at room temperature
generous ¼ cup (75 ml)	soy milk
1⅔ cups (200 g)	all-purpose flour, sifted
1 tsp	baking powder (sodium bicarbonate)
½ tsp	sea salt
	sesame seeds, toasted, or cumin seeds (optional)
	freshly ground black pepper (optional)

Using a mixer, whip the ghee or butter and stir in the soy milk. In a separate bowl, combine the flour, baking powder, and salt. Little by little, add the dry ingredients, including spices or seeds, if desired. Form the dough into a ball, cover with plastic wrap (cling film), and place in the refrigerator for 1 hour.

Preheat the oven to 350°F/180°C/Gas Mark 4. Roll out the dough to a thickness of ⅛ inch (2 mm) and cut out 1½ inch (4 cm) squares by hand or use a cookie cutter. Bake for 10 minutes or until very lightly browned. Serve with Apple-Apricot Chutney (see page 238) or butter and cheese.

Puréed Apricot with Vanilla Beans   Makes approximately 1 quart (1 liter)

3¼ lb (1.5 kg)	ripe apricots, halved and pitted (stoned)
1¾ cups (350 g)	superfine (caster) sugar
1	vanilla bean, sliced lengthwise
1	lemon, juiced

Set the fruit in a large, heavy-bottom pot. Pour the sugar on top and leave the fruit to macerate overnight in a cool place.

On the following day, place the pot with the macerated apricots over medium heat, add the vanilla bean and lemon juice, and stir constantly until the sugar dissolves. Increase the heat to medium-high, and, while stirring, boil off the liquid. Remove the vanilla bean and blend the mixture using an immersion hand blender. Cook for another 5 minutes and pour into a sterilized jar (see page 238).

Note
This goes very well with Azuki Bean Paste (see page 318), Soy Milk Jelly with Black Sugar Syrup (see page 318), or vanilla ice cream. In summer, it can also be used to make a very nice Bellini cocktail with dry sparkling or white wine.

Fresh Garden Pickles — Makes 4 medium preserving jars

Adapted from *Delia's How to Cook, Book Three*

3 medium	red onions, cut into thin wedges
3 medium	zucchini, cut into thick rounds
1 medium	fennel, cut into wedges
2 medium	red peppers, coarsely chopped
2 medium	yellow peppers, coarsely chopped
2 medium	carrots, cut into thick matchsticks
2 handfuls	mushrooms
6 oz (175 g)	sea salt
6 cloves	garlic, thinly sliced
7 TB	olive oil
8	bay leaves
8 small sprigs	rosemary
8 small sprigs	thyme
3–3½ cups (750–850 ml)	white wine vinegar
16	black peppercorns
8	small dried red chiles

The night before pickling, prepare your vegetables by arranging them in layers in a nonmetallic bowl. Make a brine by whisking the salt into 7¼ cups (1.75 liters) cold water, and pour this over the vegetables. Cover the vegetables with a plate, place a weight on top to keep them submerged, and leave overnight.

The following day, drain the brine; rinse the vegetables well, and pat dry.

Sterilize the jars (see page 238).

Put the vegetables into a bowl and mix in the garlic and olive oil. Drop a bay leaf, a sprig of rosemary, and a sprig of thyme into the bottom of each of the hot sterilized jars, and pour a small amount of vinegar over. Then add in the vegetables, putting in the remaining herbs, peppercorns, and chiles as you go. Pour in enough vinegar so the vegetables are completely covered. Jiggle the jars to ensure that no air is trapped inside, pushing the vegetables down firmly under the liquid before you screw on vinegar-proof lids. Label and store the jars in a cool, dry place for about 1 month before eating. The jars will keep for up to 6 months.

Preserving techniques allow us to capture both the sweet and the savory sides of one season's produce and save them for a time of year when those flavors might be harder to find. There is a special pleasure in finding a jar of summer on the studio table in the middle of February.

Sterilizing Preserving Jars

To sterilize, wash the jars and lids thoroughly with hot soapy water and then rinse in warm water, making sure that the lids are without dents or rust. Immerse the jars in cold water in a large pot, bring to a boil, and leave the jars in the boiling water for 5 minutes. Carefully transfer the jars, facing head-down, to a counter lined with a clean dish (tea) towel. (Alternatively, arrange the jars on a baking sheet (tray) and place in a preheated 350°F/180°C/Gas Mark 4 oven for 5 minutes.) While the jars are still hot, add their contents, which should also be hot. Adding cold contents to a hot jar can break the glass.

Apple-Apricot Chutney Makes 4–5 small preserving jars

1 lb 3 oz (550 g)	apples, chopped
7 oz (200 g)	dried apricots, coarsely chopped
1¾ oz (50 g)	raisins
6 cloves	garlic, crushed
4 TB	fresh ginger, finely chopped
1⅔ cups (400 ml)	apple vinegar
2 cups (400 g)	sugar
2 tsp	sea salt
½ tsp	cayenne pepper

Sterilize the jars.

Place all ingredients in a heavy-bottom saucepan and bring to a boil. Reduce the heat and simmer for about 30 minutes until the chutney reaches a jam-like consistency. Pour hot chutney into sterilized jars, closing them firmly. Store in the pantry for up to 3 years.

Elderflower Cordial Makes 5 medium bottles

By Gerit Bünnig, artist and friend of the studio

50	elderflower heads
9 lb (4 kg)	sugar
3–6	lemons, juiced
3 oz (80 g)	citric acid
1 gallon (3.5 liters)	water

By hand, gently clean the flower heads to remove any small insects; don't wash them, as this will weaken their flavor. Combine the sugar, lemon juice, and citric acid with 1 gallon (3.5 liters) water in a large pot and bring to a boil. Immediately remove from heat and add the flower heads. Cover and leave in a cool, dark place to steep for 1 week.

Pour the mixture through a fine strainer (sieve), boil it again, and then pour it while hot into sterilized bottles. Close firmly.

(Elderflower cordial can be served in a cocktail with white wine or prosecco, or simply mixed with sparkling water.)

By Sachiko Iwama
and Yoshito Watanabe

Umeboshi   Makes 22½ lb (10 kg) umeboshi and 1 quart (1 liter) ume su

22½ lb (10 kg)	ume plums, ripe (yellowish but not too soft)
generous 2 cups (500 ml) . . .	syochu (or comparable distilled spirits, 35% alcohol by volume)
3¼ lb (1.5 kg)	unrefined sea salt (10–15% of total mass of ume fruits)
4½ lb (2 kg)	red shiso leaves already salted and pressed
Also needed	two heavy weights (45 lb/ 20 kg in total), a number of flat, woven baskets, and a 4 gallon (15-liter) nonmetal container with a removable inner lid. A partly perforated wooden or plastic plate can be fitted to this purpose. Because of the high acidity of the ume, it is best to use as few metallic kitchen utensils as possible when making this recipe.

Umeboshi, a pickled plum, is one of many heavily salted, fermented fruits in Japanese cuisine. "These salty and sour fruits are used as both seasoning and medicine in Japan. Aveline Kushi, the Japanese author of several macrobiotic cookbooks, recounts a Japanese adage: 'Eat one umeboshi plum before taking a journey and you will have a safe trip.' The ume-plums are harvested green, not fully ripe. The red color of umeboshi plums comes from the leaf of perilla, also known as beefsteak plant, or 'shiso' in Japanese." (Sandor Ellix Katz, *The Art of Fermentation*)

Clean and dry the container, inner lid, and weights, and sterilize them with alcohol. Very carefully wash the ume and dry with a clean towel. Be careful not to scratch any skin of the ume, and remove any blemishes or scratches as they lead to mold growing, which will cause your umeboshi to fail.

Pour some of the syochu in a bowl and roll the ume in it. This both allows the ume to absorb salt and sterilizes them. Arrange some of the ume in the container to create a layer one ume deep; sprinkle sea salt on top. Make a second layer and sprinkle with salt. Repeat with plums and salt, gradually increasing the amount of salt with each successive layer. Cover the last layer of ume completely with salt.

Pour 1 cup of syochu down the inside walls of the container. This prevents the ume from molding and helps draw water out faster. Place the inner lid on the top layer of the salted ume and the weights on top of the lid.

Wrap the container in newspaper and tie it with a string.

After 4 to 5 days, the level of the liquid in the container (white ume vinegar or "ume su") will be higher than the top layer of the ume. When this happens, reduce the weight by half, reset the inner lid, and wrap again in paper. After an additional 5 to 6 days, pour some of the ume su into a clean bottle, bringing the liquid level in the container about 1 inch (2 to 3 cm) below the top of the ume. Uniformly spread red shiso leaves over the salted ume, place the weights back on the inner lid, and let the container sit for at least 2 weeks.

On a hot and dry summer day, with the weather outlook forecasting at least 4 consecutive sunny days, begin the following process in the morning:

1st day
Set woven flat baskets on rests, making sure that the undersides can breathe. Separate the ume from the red shiso leaves.

Arrange the ume in flat baskets and let them dry in the sun. Squeeze the shiso dry, break them into pieces, and spread in separate baskets, letting them dry in the sun. Pour the ume su into a bowl and place it, uncovered, in the sun. Halfway through the day, turn the ume.

In the evening, return the dried ume and shiso back to the ume su while it is still warm. This process makes the skins of the ume moist and soft.

2nd day
Arrange the ume and the shiso again in their respective baskets in the sun. Halfway through the day, turn the ume. Filter the ume su and store it in a bottle. In the evening, bring the baskets with the ume and shiso inside.

3rd day
Bring the baskets back into the sun, turn the ume halfway through the day, and then bring the baskets back inside in the evening.

4th day
Bring the baskets back into the sun and turn the ume halfway through the day. In the evening, put all the ume into clean jars and store them at room temperature. The shiso leaves can be stored in the refrigerator as they are, or ground into a powder called *yukari*.

If the salt content is greater than 17 percent of the weight of the ume, no mold will form; if the salt added is less than 10 percent of the weight of the ume, mold grows easily. Therefore, err on the side of using more salt rather than less.

Make sure to thoroughly sterilize all utensils and containers when preparing umeboshi.

The weights used should be at least twice the mass of the ume, so that the plums release their liquid as quickly as possible.

When Al joined the studio, he began making variations of this chile sauce, a homage to his friend Skinny.

Skinny's Tuff Gong Blaze Makes 3 small preserving jars

By Al Laufeld

1 lb 2 oz (500 g)	scotch bonnet peppers
5 cloves	garlic
1 bunch	scallions (spring onions)
1 bunch	thyme
1¼ cups (300 ml)	peanut oil
. . . .	salt
. . . .	latex gloves for cutting the chiles

On the way back from Port Antonio Market to your hillside Blue Mountain abode, stop by the vegetable garden and collect a bagful of ingredients: grab some garlic, and scallions, thyme, and a righteous amount of peppers from your scotch bonnet patch (in lieu of a Jamaican retreat, your local farmers' market will do).

Fire up the hi-fi and start off with a nice round of rocksteady along the lines of Alton Ellis or Otis Gayle. Finely chop the scotch bonnets, garlic, scallions, and thyme. Heat up a large saucepan until hot and add peanut oil to cover the base. Cook the peppers, scallions, and garlic at high heat for about 3 minutes until they're slightly browned. Switch the sound system over to something like Lee Perry or Horace Andy. Turn the heat down to low and add the thyme and salt. Leave the pan at this temperature and stir frequently for 20 minutes. Remove from heat and let your sauce cool down to some Sugar Minott.

Best used to jerk a freshly caught red snapper, clad in aluminium foil and cooked in your campfire. Store in a sterilized jar (see page 238).

The kitchen was inspired to make a batch of hot sauce after the chiles from the rooftop garden weren't being used frequently enough in the daily dishes. Thórdís and Aykan filled a few bowls with red, green, and purple peppers and turned them into a huge jar of homemade hot sauce.

Studio Garden Chile Sauce Makes about 6 cups (1.5 liters)

By Aykan Safoğlu and Thórdís Magnea Jónsdóttir

4½ lb (2 kg)	tabasco or long red hot peppers, seeded and finely sliced
6 cloves	garlic
3 TB	sea salt
6 tsp	horseradish, finely grated
2½ pints (1.4 liters)	apple cider or wine vinegar
. . . .	gloves for cutting the chiles

Sterilize the jars (see page 238). Heat a large, heavy-bottom saucepan and add the peppers, garlic, and 1 cup of water. Simmer until tender and then process in a blender until smooth. Do not breathe in the fumes from the pan or blender.

Return the blended chiles to the pan, add the remaining ingredients, and simmer until tender, stirring to blend.

Pour the sauce carefully into hot, sterilized 16-ounce (½ liter) jars and close firmly. Store in a cool place for up to 3 years.

Kimchi   Makes about 11 lb (4–5 kg)

11 lb (5 kg)	Chinese cabbage (napa cabbage)
7 oz (200 g)	sea salt, plus more as needed
4½ lb (2 kg)	daikon radishes, cut into matchsticks
10 bunches	scallions (spring onions), chopped

For the paste

5 TB	honey
1 head	garlic, pounded into paste
1 hand-size piece	fresh ginger, peeled and finely grated
3½ oz (100 g)	ground kombu (can be substituted with kombu or wakame strips)
20 TB	ground paprika
1 TB	chili powder
. . . .	latex gloves to apply the paste

Prepare the vegetables
Lightly wash the cabbage. Cut any remaining part of the stem from the base of the cabbage heads, making sure not to cut into the leaves. The head should remain intact. Cut a cross into the base, about 1½ inches (4 cm) deep. From the center of this cross, pull the cabbage apart into halves lengthwise. Pull apart each of the halves, to make quarters. When all the heads have been quartered, place the salt in a bowl and use your fingertips to gently pry apart the leaves (still attached to the core). Massage salt onto both sides of each leaf. Apply more salt to the thick bases of the leaves where they meet the core. Let cabbage sit in a large bowl for 5 hours. Without squeezing, allow the cabbage to drain in a colander until all the brine has drained.

Combine the daikon and scallions in a large bowl and toss with salt. When the cabbage is completely drained, place in a separate bowl.

Make the paste
Place the honey, garlic, ginger, kombu, paprika, and chili powder in a food processor fitted with a blade. Blend until a thick paste forms. (If using dried seaweed strips instead of ground, first soak the strips in cold water.

Once kombu is soft, drain [you can reserve the brine for a soup stock], add to the food processor, and blend with the other ingredients.)

Finish
Add one third of the paste to the daikon-scallion mixture. Using your gloved hands, stir and squeeze the paste into the vegetables until thoroughly combined and evenly coated. Take another third of the paste and rub it into each cabbage leaf in the same way you did with the salt, again with more paste at the base and less on the delicate tops. When all cabbage quarters have been coated, stuff the radish mixture between the cabbage leaves in the same manner. Save the remaining paste for another use. If you prefer more heat and spice, you can use half instead of a third of the paste for each step, or adjust the recipe according to taste.

Place everything in one container. Press down on the kimchi to remove any pockets of air. Cover with a lid or towel and let sit at room temperature for 1 day. Store kimchi in the refrigerator for up to 1 month. It will mature to its best flavor after 1 or 2 weeks. (It is delicious when it is fermented and sour as sauerkraut. We use the kimchi in fried rice dishes, omelets, and soups.)

Shiitake Stock   Makes a generous 2 quarts (2 liters)

12 . . . . dried shiitake mushrooms

Soak the shiitakes in 2 quarts (2 liters) water overnight. In a large pot set over medium heat, bring the mushrooms slowly to a boil in their soaking water; remove them from heat. Drain the shiitakes and reserve the stock. The stock should be refrigerated.

Note
The leftover shiitakes can be prepared and served with rice. In a saucepan, combine the sliced shiitakes with 3 tablespoons shoyu soy sauce and 1 teaspoon black sugar. Mirin or sake can also be added, as can fresh grated ginger. Cook over medium heat until all of the liquid has evaporated.

Broccoli and Barley
with Parsley
see page 153

Carrot and Radicchio
Garden Salad
see page 353

Quinoa with Arugula and Oyster Mushrooms   Serves 6 | 60

9 oz (250 g) | 5½ lb (2.5 kg) . . . quinoa
1 | 8 . . . . lemon/s, juiced and zested
. . . . olive oil
. . . . sea salt and freshly ground
                           black pepper
9 oz (250 g) | 5½ lb (2.5 kg) . . . oyster mushrooms, cleaned
2 | 15 cloves . . . . garlic, crushed
4¼ oz (125 g) | 2½ lb (1.25 kg) . . arugula (rocket), blanched
1 | 8 bunch/es . . . . flat-leaf parsley, chopped

Rinse and drain the quinoa. Place in a pan, add a generous 2 cups (500 ml) or 1⅓ gallons (5 liters) water, and bring to a boil. Cover, reduce heat to low, and simmer for 10 minutes. Remove from heat as soon as the water has been absorbed, stir once, and cover with a clean kitchen (tea) towel. The quinoa should swell but still have a little bite. Add the lemon juice and zest, a little olive oil, and salt and pepper to taste.

Gently pull the mushrooms into strips. In a heavy-bottom skillet, heat some olive oil and cook the mushrooms with garlic and salt until they are lightly browned.

Gently combine the quinoa, mushrooms, and arugula. Season with salt and pepper, and garnish with parsley before serving.

Variations
The mushrooms can be substituted with various other vegetables. Our favorites are broccoli, spinach, and cauliflower.

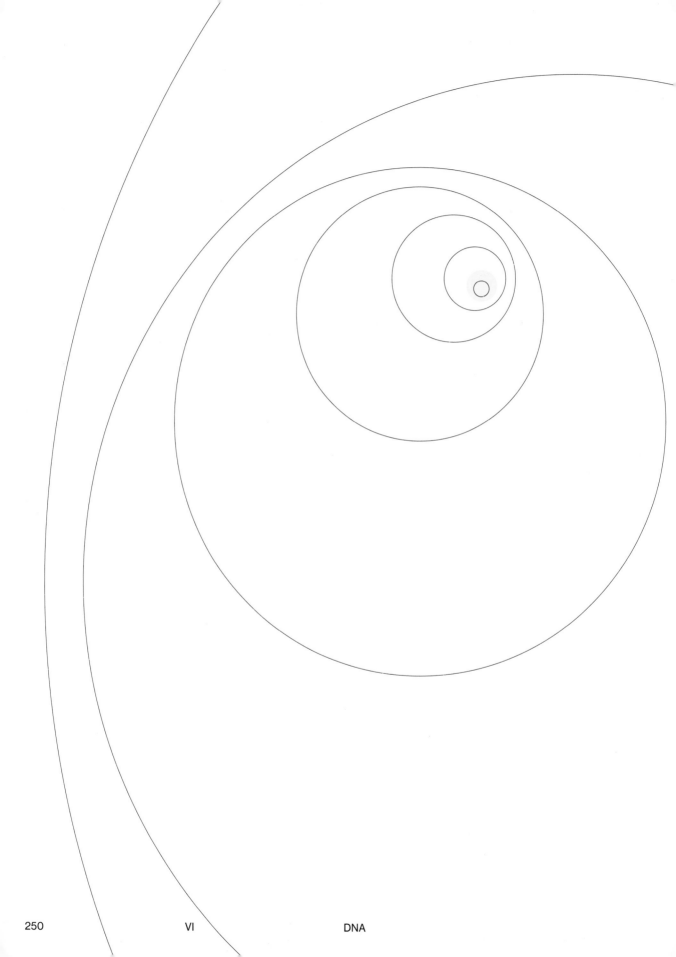

       DNA

DNA

Asako Iwama and
Lauren Maurer

DNA masterminds all bio-chemical processes, in plants and animals alike. Two spiral strands winding around each other make up the iconic double helix: it contains the encoded genetic information that allows living organisms to develop, replicate, and function. Considering that these spirals are crucial to our health, how can we support their functioning through the choices we make in our kitchen?

One approach that has influenced our cooking and understanding of food is macrobiotics, which puts great emphasis on complementary foods, or the principle of opposites. Macrobiotics combines foods so that they interact with each other: sweet and salty, cool and hot – or, in other words, yin and yang. Meals prepared and eaten according to these principles are thought to maintain or adjust the body and its needs in different conditions: from external conditions, like seasons and the weather, to the internal conditions of our organism, which macrobiotic philosophy considers to be not static but in motion and to

include phases of balance and imbalance. Central to macrobiotics are foods like whole grains, green and root vegetables, seaweed, fish, nuts, beans, and tofu. On a daily basis, these foods form the backbone of our cooking in the studio, even though we don't keep a strictly macrobiotic kitchen.

We are aware of the importance of maintaining the precious balance and strength of our organism. To us, this awareness raises the question of responsibility in a universe where, the closer you look, the more you see that everything is intricately linked to the larger whole. What we do or don't do has undeniable effects. We feel that questions of responsibility

should also be asked with regard to the intentional modification of genetic material. Increasingly, crops like corn or soy are being genetically modified to yield greater profits, while long-term effects on the biosphere remain unclear. Motives, without a doubt, vary greatly, but we must not forget that touching any strand of a tensely stretched net will resonate throughout its entirety.

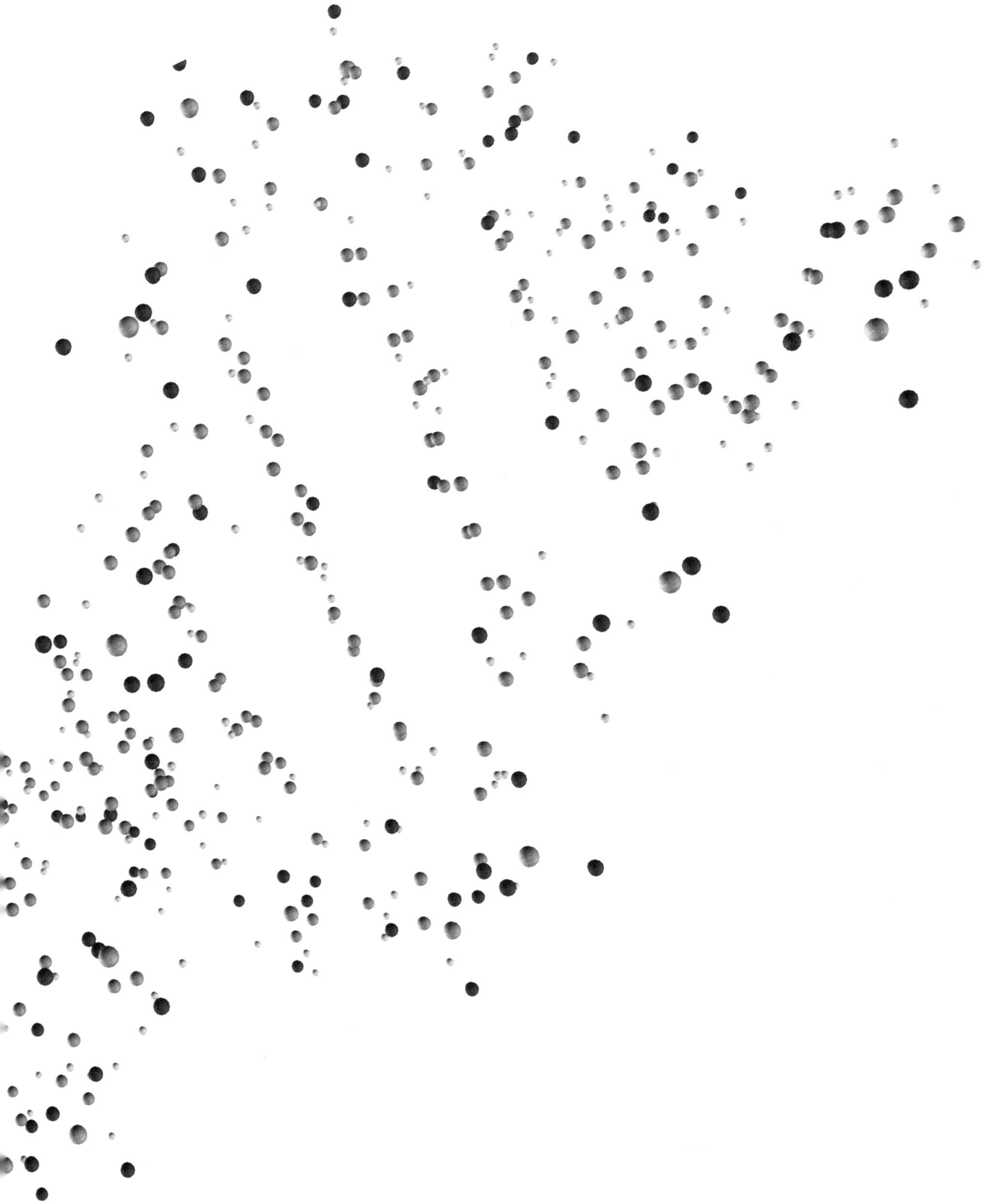

"The most common pattern found in nature and all phenomena is the spiral. We see it in every day patterns; autumn leaves headed toward the ground in a spirallic freefall; the helical form of DNA and RNA; the rings of a seashell, exhaust smoke coming out of a car, sound waves, etc. Within the move-ment of a spiral, there is always a return near the place of origin, but in a more evolved direction. Our personal growth parallels this movement; we get better, we get worse, we get better, we get worse. Growth is rarely linear. No one just, 'gets better.' Often, it's getting worse that becomes our best teacher and enables us to recover. This give us a point of measurability toward seeing a larger picture."

Verne Varona
A Guide to the Macrobiotic Principles

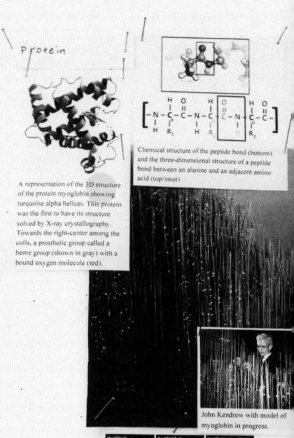

Protein

A representation of the 3D structure of the protein myoglobin showing turquoise alpha helices. This protein was the first to have its structure solved by X-ray crystallography. Towards the right-center among the coils, a prosthetic group called a heme group (shown in gray) with a bound oxygen molecule (red).

Chemical structure of the peptide bond (bottom) and the three-dimensional structure of a peptide bond between an alanine and an adjacent amino acid (top/inset)

John Kendrew with model of myoglobin in progress.

DNA

DNA
RNA
V H L T P E E K   protein

e DNA sequence of a gene encodes
amino acid sequence of a protein.

RNA

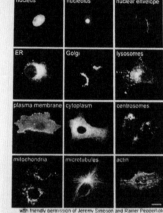

nucleus	nucleolus	nuclear envelope
ER	Golgi	lysosomes
plasma membrane	cytoplasm	centrosomes
mitochondria	microtubules	actin

with friendly permission of Jeremy Simpson and Rainer Pepperkok

Proteins in different cellular compartments and structures tagged with green fluorescent protein (here, white)

Resonan
individu

Molecul
compara
immuno
insulin
and glu

/enzymes/

Dna (amino acids, proteins, enzymes, radiatio

/amino acids

of the peptide bond that links
ds to form a protein polymer

several proteins showing their
rom left to right are:
IgG, an antibody), hemoglobin,
adenylate kinase (an enzyme),
etase (an enzyme).

Cytosine

Guanine

Adenine

Thymine

A.   B.

1   2   3   4   5

© 2006 Merriam-Webster, Inc.

"the seed is as much part of the relationship with the bee and the butterfly as it is with the soil
organisms that it ultimately sustains, as it is with the food that we eat. All these relationships
are in the seed.". "With commercialization as the objective, reductionism became the
criterion of scientific validity."

"The agricultural paradigm has been reduced to a monoculture of commodities. They can't
produce more commodities - but they can produce more food."...

Vandana Shiva in Documenta Notes

Cellula   DNA

Nucleo   Cromosoma

255

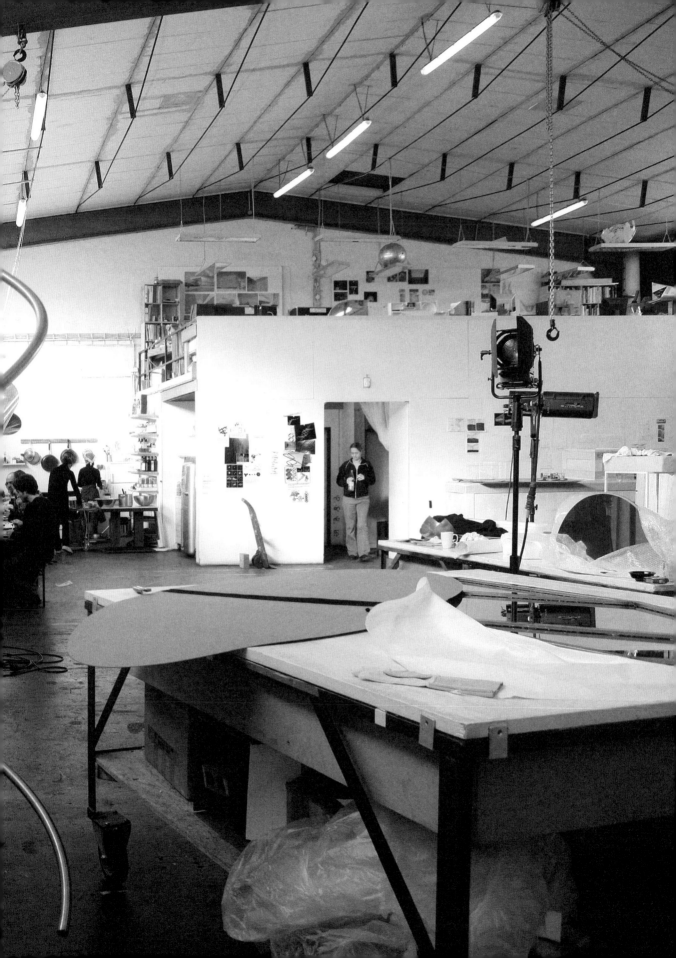

Olafur Eliasson
Colour spiral, 2005

Jeremias Holliger, participant in the Institut für Raumexperimente

J: When I first saw the book *Demokratie? Eine Debatte* (*Democracy in What State?*), I was curious about Jean-Luc Nancy's essay because I had already read parts of his text *The Confronted Community* on different occasions, some passages alone, some in small groups, some in a larger group of people. I assumed his text on democracy would connect to what I was interested in: the question of community. But when I opened the book, I found myself confronted with an unreadable print of Nancy's text. Two voices crossed each other in the book, so to speak!

A: But why an unreadable text about democracy in a cookbook?

J: Well – because I can see a recipe in it.

A: A recipe for what?

J: I think it can function as a recipe for thinking.

A: A recipe for how to think about thinking?

J: Yes!

A: Within that thinking about thinking, doesn't it also address the question of how to think about community?

J: Absolutely. Thinking seems to take place at the periphery of any community, so to speak, on an individual level. Yet this radically decentralized process creates a communal body of thought. Through the process of communication, individuals constitute a community.

A: So thinking neither belongs to someone, nor is it something in itself.

J: Right. It only exists through different, radically separate coproducers, who, at the same time, come into existence only by virtue of that thinking community.

A: How does this relate to the text?

J: First, I think we have to ask ourselves if the object we see is still a text.

A: For me, it is a borderline case – it's interesting to think what it might open up. How do you see it?

J: It is a gift, in the first place. That's how I felt when I first found the book with an unreadable text in it. At the same time that it is a gift, the text seemed to imply an underdeveloped ability on the reader's part; it seemed to call for the development of a skill for un-reading. And yet it seemed an almost generous gesture in providing me with a tool to work on that almost aggressively unreadable text.

A: So it's a recipe as well as a tool. But how can we work with it? What can we do with it?

J: Looking at it, we initially feel lost. We can't hold onto any word or thing. We lose our "wording," so to speak. But even if the text seems to offer less than an ordinary text, this lack is something we can appreciate for the moment.

A: It confronts us with an almost overwhelming nothingness!

J: Yes, indeed, but in a way this could happen all the time, in any context, even when we seem to have much more to hold on to.

A: You mean we just assume we can hold on to something, but in fact our existence is far more groundless.

J: Right! Now the recipe comes into play. It is a model for putting things into relation with each other.

A: As an example, you might say, when we mix an egg with sugar, it's not only about the cake we want to make, but first of all about the egg and the sugar and their specific relationship.

J: In a way, it's about trust, yes!

A: The trust that egg and sugar will make a cake, associating with each other in their own way?

J: Yes, but without a cake pan, the egg and sugar might not connect.

A: Which does not necessarily mean that the pan makes the cake.

J: No. The form gives the ingredients space to develop their interplay, but it does not define them.

A: In fact, this is a political question.

J: True, I think this is how the recipe could be read too.

A: I like reading this unreadable text with you. Is there another layer of meaning you can see?

J: Yes, in a way it is a metaphor for communication. For instance, when you hear someone saying something and you don't go into what is being said but into the fact that there are things being said. Maybe also into the way things are said. You start by listening. You pay attention to the very fact of voices appearing, trying to communicate.

A: You need silence to listen in such a way. Would you say that silence is the essence of our tool?

J: Normally we go straight to the meaning and purpose of what is being said. Silence can be a tool to go beyond.

A: An active silence, so to speak, because it means hearing the other. The silence you propose is the closed, chewing mouth of that one thinking community.

A fictional conversation between Jeremias Holliger (J) and Asako Iwama (A)

'pheu
ô
ioh
oi
oi moi
ai ai
otototoi
èè
e
he-e
euoi
euai
i-uh'*

* Wolfgang Schadewaldt, *Antikes Drama auf dem Theater heute,* Pfullingen: Neske, 1969, p. 25

Overleaf:
Jeremias Holliger,
UN - READ - ABILITY, 2013

[...] dem Bedürfnis nach einem Ver-
[...] die Aufnahme – ohne daß damit eine Verherrli-
chung [...] die Aufgabe [...]
[...] dieses Syn-
tagma in dieser Weise zu zweckentfremden ...) Politik ist, die
Eröffnung von Sphären zu ermöglichen, die einer anderen
Ordnung folgen. Es handelt sich dabei um die Sphären der
Wahrheit und des Sinns, welche durch die Ausdrücke »Kunst«,
[...] möglichen
[...] darin, die Bewahrung gesellschaftlicher Stabi-
lität [...]

Frage nach dem Sinn oder der Wahrheit des Miteinanders.

Der Kommunismus war also nicht politisch, und er mußte es auch nicht sein. Seine Kritik an der Absonderung der Politik war selbst nicht politisch. Der Kommunismus hat dies nicht gewußt, doch wir sollten es jetzt wissen.

[...] auch Physiokratie oder Mediokratie [...]

[...] solche Verurteilung hinaus). Eine [...]

A Sticky Recipe: My Contribution to a Saint Society

Nico Dockx, artist-writer-curator-publisher

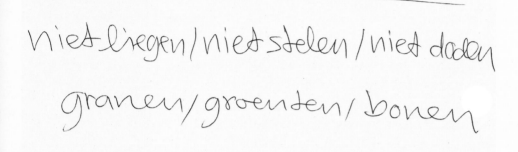

no lying / no stealing / no killing
grains / vegetables / beans
12.12.2010
© Pictoright, Louwrien Wijers

Whenever someone else comes into the kitchen to help or to eat with you, the conversation changes. Therefore, I have decided to contribute here a recipe not just for cooking but for holding things together, for sitting together – perhaps like rice, which becomes sticky when slowly boiled in hot water. A sticky recipe for bringing together that which cannot always be joined. Why should we want to persecute ourselves with this question of where it all comes from and where it is all leading? Insight is something that happens at the point of our discontinuity, when we have to let go in order for other things to come. Improvisation. We have to cook it up fresh each time. To let ourselves be touched. It is felt. Inspired and inspiring. This recipe should be a kind of energy that is not visual or descriptive; it is just there and its presence makes the difference in space. It has this capacity of changing habits, appetites, and minds. And we know very well that we want nothing more than to be transformed. It sticks. Its creativity is in the moment. It is a dialog with the moment; it has no time. It is a search, like looking for mushrooms. It is something that is balancing, which behaves like the body, and which has breathing aspects and counterpoised weights. It is the appearance of what is not entirely there yet. It is an echo of unfinished business. It is liquid and compassionate, seeking no directions. It is like cooking some raw ingredients into a nice and healthy meal. I have found food to be a common medium for creating situations where things and experiences can happen and for communicating that which does not always entail language but has a spiritual dimension. The best investment is to give to the world and not to take from it. Moving, not keeping. I like the idea of passage, like passing something. I like to pass something to somebody else. In this communal act of cooking and eating together, I hope it is possible to cross some of our physical and imaginary boundaries and produce new conversations that have neither an ostensible target nor purpose, but are just listening. If we cannot think and talk together, then we cannot do anything together. Letting the other in requires trust, understanding, patience, generosity, and the ability to receive. This, in fact, may be one of the most difficult, yet powerful, aspects of experience because it entails intense self-examination and commitment on the part of everyone involved. Metabolism has been a property of life since it began, since our very beginning. It engages – it is engagement. It entangles and unravels. It is dangerous to occupy territory. In my view, art is a chemical reactive that, propagating through contagion, can interfere with the molecular composition of the various environments it enters, dissolving its toxic elements. I feel we have to teach and learn with our behavior, rejecting all categories of fixed thought – and not create frozen images, but spatial, color, and light conditions. We are in the air, in the climate. It is ongoing, and it acts on our skin. What goes on in our innermost being is worth all our love; this is what we must work on however we can and not waste too much time and energy on clarifying our attitude to others. When I was making the first bead (that is how I see a work, an event), I had no idea what the necklace would be. It was only when I saw all of them in one string that I could understand all the beauty of it.

06.05.2013

Sticky Rice, Institut für
Raumexperimente, Berlin,
October 26–28, 2011

The Sticky Rice workshop took place October 26–28, 2011, at the Institut für Raumexperimente. A collaborative, educational encounter between the institute and guests from the Royal Academy of Fine Arts in Antwerp, Belgium, the workshop formed part of a series of events initiated by artist Nico Dockx and based on material from the archives of artist Louwrien Wijers. The event revolved around material from two conferences organized by Wijers, in 1990 and 1996, both titled "Art Meets Science and Spirituality in a Changing Economy." As an important part of the workshop, participants reedited a 1989 interview between Wijers and neuroscientist Francisco J. Varela. His idea that "what we do and what we see is not separate", taken from the interview, came to link conversations that took place at Sticky Rice between Wijers and guests, like curator and writer Sarat Maharaj and artist Rirkrit Tiravanija. It also informed a food experiment performed by artist and cook Egon Hanfstingl, together with Asako Iwama and Lauren Maurer. Based on the idea of "eating whole foods," Iwama, Maurer, and Hanfstingl used all parts of the ingredients that went into the dishes, including the residue of soybeans usually discarded after making soy milk and tofu.

Contemporary scientific research agrees that whole grains contain more nutritional value than milled and refined grain products. Nonetheless, industrial millers reduce wheat grains, for instance, by 40 to 50 percent in order to sell the fiber to the pharmaceutical and animal food industry. The impoverished flour is then presented to the badly informed consumer. Through my food experiments at the Sticky Rice workshop, I tried to create awareness of these facts by (re) introducing the idea of eating whole foods.

Eating all parts of the plants and animals that are digestible and properly prepared for consumption feeds all parts of the human body. Complete food makes a body and a mind that can connect more easily to the "whole" — our surroundings, the universe. The quality of your blood is defined by the quality of the food you take in: you are your own creator.

In 1796, the German medical doctor Christoph Wilhelm Hufeland published his bestselling book *Macrobiotics: The Art of Prolonging Human Life,* in which he coined the term "macrobiotics," advocating his understanding of food and life. About two centuries later, the Japanese doctor Sagen Ishizuka developed his theory, also calling it macrobiotics, on the complementary effects of sodium (Na) and potassium (K) as yin and yang elements that influence human health. In 1912, the Japanese philosopher George Ohsawa studied Ishizuka's findings intensively and promoted macrobiotics — notably in Japan and in Europe, where he lived for many years — as a system to reach absolute health. He advocated eating 50 percent grains, 30 percent vegetables, 10 percent beans, and 10 percent of any other food of choice. The macrobiotic concept went from West to East and back to the West. It informed the food experiments performed at the Sticky Rice workshop, bringing together Eastern and Western perspectives in both ingredients and philosophy.

Egon Hanfstingl, artist and cook

These recipes were prepared by Egon Hanfstingl for the Sticky Rice event. Egon writes: "The burdock used in this recipe is a cultivated root of a well-known common herb, at least in Germany, whose burr-like seeds stick to dogs and sweaters. Long known for its strengthening and cleansing properties, it is a very *yang* and earthy plant, which helps to keep the feet on the ground. I love to add some lemon peel to the cooking water to give it a little lightness. This recipe is a simple, elegant, and traditional Japanese recipe."

Burdock with Sesame — Serves 6 | 60

2	20	burdock roots (or black salsify), 8–12 inches (20–30 cm) long
1 TB	⅔ cup (150 ml)	toasted sesame oil
4–5 TB	2½–3 cups (600–750 ml)	shoyu soy sauce
3 TB	3 cups (350 g)	toasted sesame seeds

By Egon Hanfstingl, adapted from *Macrobiotic Cuisine*

Scrub the burdock with a natural fiber brush and cut into long segments that just fit into your skillet. Cook the burdock in oil until its strong aroma is no longer released. Add just enough water to cover the burdock, and bring to a boil. Reduce heat to low and cover the pan. Cook until burdock is tender and no longer resistant to a fork or skewer. Add water during cooking if necessary. Add soy sauce and simmer until all of the liquid is evaporated. Cut the burdock into ¾-inch (2 cm) pieces and serve upright, topped with toasted sesame seeds.

Lotus Root and Onion Pakoras with Raita Dip — Serves 6 | 60

By Egon Hanfstingl

For the Pakora

7 oz (200 g)	4½ lb (2 kg)	chickpea flour
1 tsp	3 TB	ground turmeric
1 tsp	3 TB	ground coriander
1 tsp	3 TB	ground cumin
1 tsp	3 TB	ground ginger
¼	2.5 tsp	ground cinnamon
⅛	1 tsp	asafoetida powder (or garlic)
⅛	1 tsp	ajwain seeds
1 tsp	3 TB	salt
1 tsp	3 TB	fresh lemon juice
	vegetable oil
5 oz (150 g)	3¼ (1.5 kg)	onions, halved and thinly sliced
5 oz (150 g)	3¼ lb (1.5 kg)	lotus roots (or fennel), halved and thinly sliced

For the Raita

2 cups (500 ml)	plain yogurt (cow or soy)
	sea salt
1½ tsp	ghee
⅛ tsp	asafoetida powder (or garlic)
1 tsp	cumin seeds

Sift the chickpea flour with the turmeric, coriander, cumin, ginger, cinnamon, and asafoetida; add ajwain and salt. Whisk in 1¼ cups (500 ml) or 3 quarts (3 liters) water and lemon juice to get a thick, smooth batter.

In a heavy-bottom saucepan, pour oil to a depth of at least 2¾ inches (7 cm) and heat to 350°F/185°C. Dip 5 to 6 pieces of the onions and lotus roots in the batter, mixing the pieces well so that they are coated, and then, one at a time, slip them into the hot oil. Fry until the vegetables are tender and the batter becomes golden brown, turning as necessary with a slotted spoon. Transfer the fried vegetables (pakoras) onto paper towels to drain. Serve immediately or keep warm under a clean towel. Repeat the process with the remaining vegetables.

Preparing the Raita
Combine the yogurt and salt in a bowl. In a small saucepan, heat the ghee and, when hot, add asafoetida and cumin and gently cook until well-toasted and fragrant. Add this sauce hot to the yogurt and immediately cover. Let stand for a few minutes then stir gently to mix. Chill and serve as a dipping sauce for the Pakoras.

Natto is a favorite dish of Asako's and very difficult to find in Berlin. The digestion of natto is aided by the naturally occurring bacteria and live cultures it contains. In Japanese cuisine, it is commonly served with rice for breakfast.

Natto

Adapted from *The Art of Fermentation*

2 lb 3 oz (1 kg)	organic straw, wheat or rice
1 lb 2 oz (500 g)	soybeans

In a large pot of water, boil the straw for 15 minutes. This will kill all bacteria except the *Bacillus subtilis* used in making natto, which can survive temperatures up to 250°F/120°C.

Wash the soybeans and put them in a bowl with four times as much water as beans. Soak for 8 hours in the summer and 14 hours in the winter. Place the soybeans and water into a saucepan and bring to a boil. Reduce heat to low and cook for about 5 hours, until the beans are very tender and easy to squish between your fingers. Add water as necessary to keep the beans just covered and stir often to keep them from burning on the bottom.

Meanwhile, make a bed of straw in a container in a place where a temperature of 104–113°F (40–45°C) can be maintained, for instance, in the oven with the pilot light or in an insulated cooler prewarmed with hot water bottles. Drain the cooked beans and spread them on the bed of straw while they are still hot, but no more than ¼ inch (5 mm) deep. Let sit for 48 hours, checking that the container stays warm. To test if the natto is ready, swirl the soybeans with chopsticks or a spoon and see if gooey strings form. Longer incubation will result in more pronounced stringiness and a more pronounced flavor.

Before adding other ingredients to the natto, mix vigorously with chopsticks until very gooey. To eat, add soy sauce, ume paste, roasted sesame seeds, scallions (spring onions), shiso, or mustard, and serve with rice.

Natto has a unique flavor and consistency and may take some time to get used to, but it contains nattokinase, which has been shown to have many health benefits, including the promotion of good blood circulation.

Tofu with Lemon Juice   Makes approximately 2¼ lb (1 kg)

1 lb 5 oz (600 g) . . . . soybeans
4 quarts and 3 cups (4.5 liters) . soft mineral or filtered water
1 cup (250 ml) . . . . fresh lemon juice

Wash the soybeans and soak in about 3½ quarts (3.5 liters) of soft mineral or filtered water. Soak for 8 hours in the summer and 14 hours in the winter. After soaking, put the beans with their water in a blender and blend for 2 minutes. Transfer to a large pot, add the remaining mineral water, and cook over medium heat, stirring constantly to keep the bottom from burning. Skim off the foam. After the mixture has come to a boil, lower the heat and simmer for 15 minutes, stirring frequently. In order to extract the soy milk from the beans, strain the mixture through a cheesecloth into a fresh pot, squeezing out all liquid while the soy is still hot.

(The leftover soy pulp is called okara and is very nutritious, containing protein and isoflavone. It can be used in many recipes or cooked together with Shiitake Stock [see page 246], soy sauce, and thinly sliced vegetables.)

Cook the soy milk over medium heat until fragrant and the temperature reaches about 160°F/70°C. Remove the pot from heat. Add half of the lemon juice, mix, and cover for 10 minutes. Add the remaining lemon juice evenly over the surface of the liquid and gently stir just

briefly. Wait 10 minutes until the soy milk has set into a sort of pudding.

Line a large sieve with a big piece of cheesecloth. Carefully transfer the curdled soy milk into the lined sieve. Fold the edges of the cheesecloth over the top and weigh down with a heavy object. Leave the weight on for 25 minutes for soft tofu, 30 minutes for medium-soft, and 35 minutes for firm tofu. When the tofu is ready, remove from the sieve and serve, or store in a container with cold water. Serve with soy sauce, freshly grated ginger, finely chopped scallions (spring onions), and toasted sesame seeds.

Note
While tofu can easily be made with lemon juice, traditionally it is made with nigari. The base of natural nigari is magnesium chloride, but it also contains over a hundred other mineral salts such as potassium chloride and calcium chloride. Nigari is derived from seawater, which has almost the same mineral balance as human blood, and may ease conditions like hay fever and eczema (atopic dermatitis). To make tofu the traditional way, replace lemon juice with ½ cup (140 ml) of liquid nigari.

Soy Yogurt   Makes about 1 quart (1 liter)

1 quart (1 liter) . . . . soy milk
2 TB . . . . soy yogurt (or ¼ tsp yogurt starter: live active bacteria [*Bifidobacterium bifidum, Lactobacillus acidophilus, Lacto-bacillus casei, Lactobacillus delbrueckii subsp bulgaricus, Lactobacillus rhamnosus, Streptococcus thermophilus*])

Heat the soy milk to between 108–113°F (42–45°C); be sure to use a thermometer to measure the temperature, as the yogurt culture can only survive in a very narrow range. Add the yogurt (or the yogurt starter) and, using a sterilized spoon, mix well. Pour

the mixture into a glass jar and place in a preheated 108–113°F (42–45°C) oven for 5 to 6 hours. Store in the refrigerator. When you are almost finished with the jar, save 2 to 3 tablespoons for your next yogurt batch.

Because more and more of the maize that is grown and sold around the world is genetically modified, it is important to us to serve organic, all-natural, and unmodified maize.

Cornbread   Serves 4–6

4 TB (60 g)	butter, melted, plus more for greasing
6 oz (180 g)	polenta
1 cup plus 2 TB (140 g)	all-purpose flour
½ tsp	sea salt
2 tsp	baking powder (sodium bicarbonate)
2	eggs
2–4 TB	honey, to taste
1 cup (240 ml)	milk

Preheat the oven to 400°F/200°C/Gas Mark 6. Grease a 9-inch (23 cm) square pan and set aside. Stir the polenta, flour, salt, and baking powder together in a large bowl. In a separate bowl, whisk together the eggs, butter, honey, and milk. Quickly mix the wet ingredients into the dry mixture, stirring until just combined. Pour batter into the pan and bake for about 25 minutes, until golden brown. Test with a toothpick – it should come out clean. Cut into squares and serve warm.

Black Bean Chili   Serves 6 | 60

11 oz (300 g)	6 lb 11 oz (3 kg)	black beans, soaked overnight
7 oz (200 g)	4½ lb (2 kg)	kidney beans, soaked overnight
4 TB	2½ cups (600 ml)	olive oil
2 medium	9 lb (4 kg)	onions, diced
2 cloves	1 head	garlic, minced
3 stalks	4 heads	celery, finely diced
1	10	red pepper/s, diced
3	20 small	dried red chiles, crumbled
1 tsp	3 TB	chipotle chile powder
1 tsp	3 TB	ground cumin
	sea salt
3 medium	6 lb 11 oz (3 kg)	carrots, diced
2	20 cans (14 oz/400 g each)	tomatoes, whole in juice
2	10	bay leaves
1 tsp	3 TB	oregano
	freshly ground black pepper
4 sprigs	4 bunches	cilantro (coriander), chopped
100 ml	1 liter	crème fraîche, whipped
	basmati rice, for serving
	Cornbread, for serving

Cover the beans with cold water and cook separately until tender, about 40 to 60 minutes. Add water as necessary to keep the beans just covered. Drain well. While the beans are cooking, heat the olive oil in a large, heavy-bottom saucepan, add the onions, and gently cook over medium heat until golden. Add the garlic, celery, peppers, chiles, chipotle powder, cumin, and a pinch of salt and continue to fry until soft, stirring to combine the flavors. Add the carrots, tomatoes, bay leaves, and salt, and bring to a boil. Reduce the heat to low and simmer for 20 minutes. Allow the sauce to thicken, stirring often to keep the bottom from burning. Add the oregano and beans to the tomatoes and cook for 10 minutes more. Season with salt and pepper to taste. Discard the bay leaves. Sprinkle chili with cilantro and serve hot with crème fraîche, basmati rice, and warm Cornbread (see above).

Red Kuri Squash Ratatouille Serves 6 | 60

1 medium |11 lb (5 kg)	eggplant/s (aubergine/s), cut into large chunks
. . . .	salt
1 | 10 large	squash, seeded and cubed
. . . .	freshly ground black pepper
. . . .	olive oil
2 medium | 9 lb (4 kg)	onions, diced
3 stalks | 4 heads	celery, stalks and leaves diced
2 | 15	small dried red chiles, crushed
3½ TB (50 ml) | 2 cups (500 ml) .	dry white wine
2 | 20 cans (14 oz /400 g each) .	whole tomatoes
2 | 20	bay leaves
2 TB | 3 bunches	thyme, finely chopped
2 TB | 3 bunches	rosemary, finely chopped
2 medium | 9 lb (4 kg)	zucchini, cut into ⅓-inch (1 cm) thick slices
2 medium | 9 lb (4 kg)	red bell peppers, cut into big chunks
2 medium | 6 lb 11 oz (3 kg) . . .	carrots, cut into big chunks
2 TB | 1¾ lb (800 g)	capers
3½ oz (100 g) | 2¼ lb (1 kg) . . .	kalamata olives
. . . .	flat-leaf parsley, chopped

Preheat the oven to 425°F/ 220°C/Gas mark 7. Sprinkle the eggplants with salt and let sit for 30 minutes, letting them release their juices. Rinse with cold water, drain well, and pat dry. Set aside.

Toss the squash in salt, pepper, and some of the olive oil, and roast on a baking sheet (tray) for 25 minutes until tender.

In a heavy-bottom saucepan, cook the onions in olive oil over medium heat until golden. Add the celery, chiles, and some salt and continue to cook, stirring until soft. Add the wine and cook until evaporated. Add the tomatoes, bay leaves, thyme and rosemary; bring to a boil; reduce heat to low, and simmer for 40 minutes.

In a heavy-bottom skillet, cook the eggplant in olive oil until lightly browned on all sides. Repeat, individually, with zucchini, red peppers, and carrots, adding a little olive oil between batches. Add the fried vegetables to the tomato sauce, and gently stir in the reserved squash.

Reduce heat and simmer, being careful not to let the vegetables get too soft. Stir in capers and olives. Taste and adjust seasonings. You should end up with a shiny, moist ratatouille with little liquid. Discard the bay leaves and garnish with parsley before serving. (Keep in mind that ratatouille tastes even better the following day.)

Spinach and Parmesan Polenta Serves 6 | 60

5 cups (1.2 liters) | 3¼ gallons (12 liters)	Vegetable Stock (see page 74) or water
11 oz (300 g) | 6 lb 11 oz (3 kg) .	polenta
3½ oz (100 g) | 2¼ lb (1 kg) . . .	butter, softened
7 oz (200 g) | 4½ lb (2 kg) . . .	parmesan, grated
11 oz (300 g) | 6 lb 11 oz (3 kg) .	spinach, blanched, drained, and puréed
. . . .	sea salt and freshly ground black pepper

Bring the vegetable stock to a simmer in a heavy-bottom large pot: it should come halfway up the side of the pan. Pour the polenta into the stock in a continuous stream, and using a long-handled whisk, whisk constantly until completely blended. The polenta will start to bubble volcanically. Reduce the heat to low and cook, stirring with a spoon to prevent a skin from forming on the top, for about 40 minutes.

The polenta is finished when it falls away from the sides of the pot. Stir in the butter, parmesan, spinach, and season with salt and pepper. Transfer to a large flat baking sheet (tray) or plate and spread out to form a cake about ¾-inch (2 cm) thick. Cool completely and then cut into slices.

Minerals

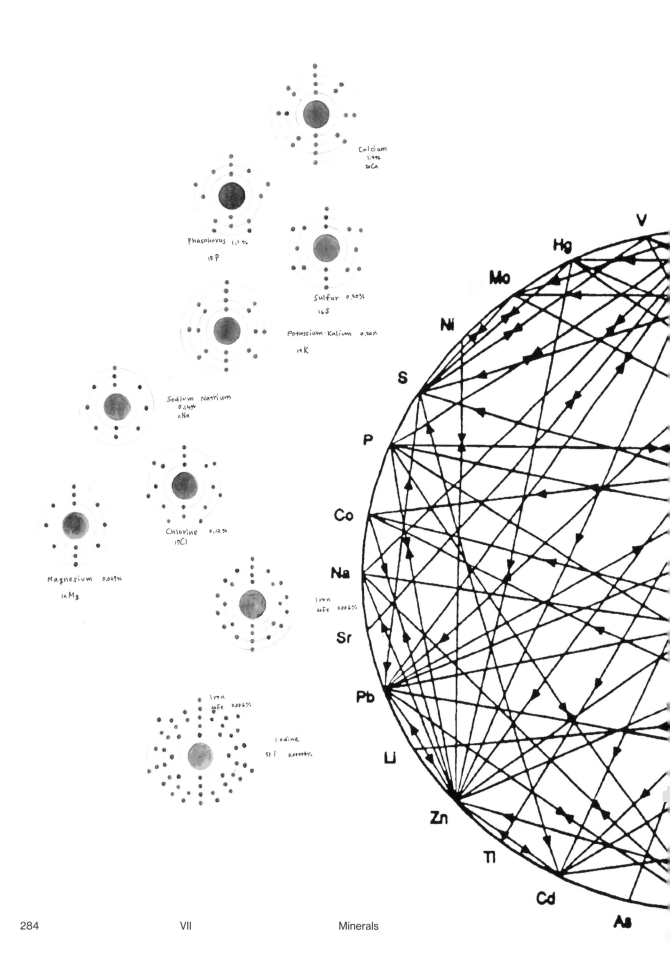

Calcium
1.4%
20Ca

Phosohorus 1,1%
15 P

Sulfur 0.20%
16 S

Potassium · Kalium 0.20%
19 K

Sodium · Natrium
0.14%
11 Na

Chlorine 0,12%
17Cl

Magnesium 0,027%
12 Mg

Iron
26Fe 0.006%

Iron
26Fe 0.006%

Iodine
53 I 0.00004%

V

Hg

Mo

Ni

S

P

Co

Na

Sr

Pb

Li

Zn

Tl

Cd

As

Minerals

Asako Iwama and
Lauren Maurer

Seaweed is an ingredient we often use in our kitchen – wakame or kombu to make stock or miso soup, wakame and hijiki prepared as salad. To us, this goes beyond a simple preference for certain foods: the vegetable from the sea is nutritious and a rich source of minerals. We generally prefer mineral-rich foods in our cooking, so we choose legumes (pulses) or brown rice over refined white rice. Tofu, which also plays an important role in many of our dishes, is a great source of calcium, magnesium, and iron. It is traditionally made with nigari, a powder extracted from seawater that contains magnesium chloride and further trace minerals.

We know that the human body needs minerals, vital nutrients it can't produce on its own. A healthy human body contains a wealth of minerals, the seven most prominent being calcium, phosphorus, potassium, sulphur, sodium, chlorine, and magnesium. Simply put, minerals are needed to support the biochemical processes of our metabolism. Calcium, for example, has beneficial effects on our bone structure, while magnesium supports the healthy functioning of muscles, heart, and blood vessels. Eating a balanced diet of foods rich in minerals creates a healthy interplay of elements within ourselves.

We are equally fascinated by the thought of minerals binding us to other habitats like water or soil; we understand them as a link to the inorganic realm. Their crystalline structures show us the beauty of atomic structures and their arrangement into intricate geometric forms. Those that are visible to the naked eye give us an inkling of the much smaller molecular structures making up everything that exists: from atoms to the universe.

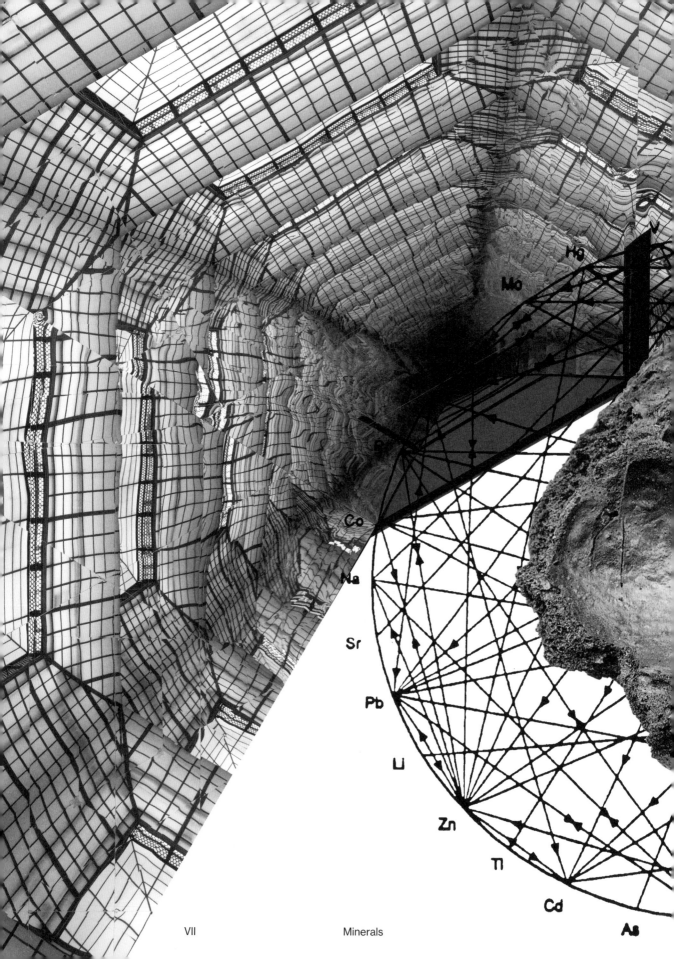

Arsenic / As

Copper / Cu

Calcite / CaCO$_3$

Fluorite / CaF$_2$

Sal Ammoniac / NH$_4$Cl

Iron / Fe

Crocoite / PbCrO$_4$

Sylvite / KCl

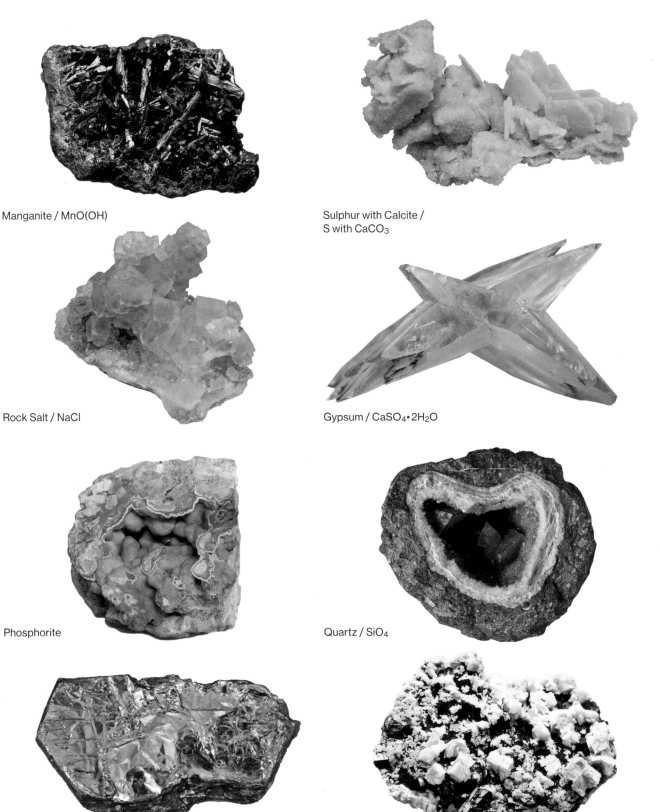

Manganite / MnO(OH)

Sulphur with Calcite /
S with CaCO$_3$

Rock Salt / NaCl

Gypsum / CaSO$_4\cdot$2H$_2$O

Phosphorite

Quartz / SiO$_4$

Molybdenite / MoS$_2$

Sphalerite with Dolomite /
ZnS with CaMg(CO$_3$)$_2$

Dietary minerals designate chemical elements required by living organisms. They do not exist outside the body in pure form except in certain cases, like iron and sulphur. The minerals above show many of these elements as they appear in nature.

Quantities of various elements
found in a human body with
a mass of 70 kg:

Calcium (Ca)	1 kg
Phosphorus (P)	780 g
Sulphur (S)	140 g
Potassium (K)	140 g
Sodium (Na)	100 g
Chlorine (Cl)	95 g
Magnesium (Mg)	19 g
Iron (Fe)	4 g
Fluorine (F)	3 g
Zinc (Zn)	2 g
Silicon (Si)	1 g
Copper (Cu)	72 mg
Iodine (I)	20 mg
Selenium (Se)	15 mg
Chromium (Cr)	14 mg
Manganese (Mn)	12 mg
Molybdenum (Mo)	0.5 mg

From "Composition of the
Human Body" Wikipedia

Olafur Eliasson, *Ice pavilion,*
1998, opening at Pfefferberg,
2010. Creamy Pink Root Soup
with Roasted Kohlrabi (see
page 162) was served at the
opening.

pp. 294–5
Ice test in the garden of the
Invalidenstrasse studio, 2003

pp. 298–9
Olafur Eliasson, *The large
Iceland series #10,* 2012

pp. 300–1
Olafur Eliasson, *The large
Iceland series #7,* 2012

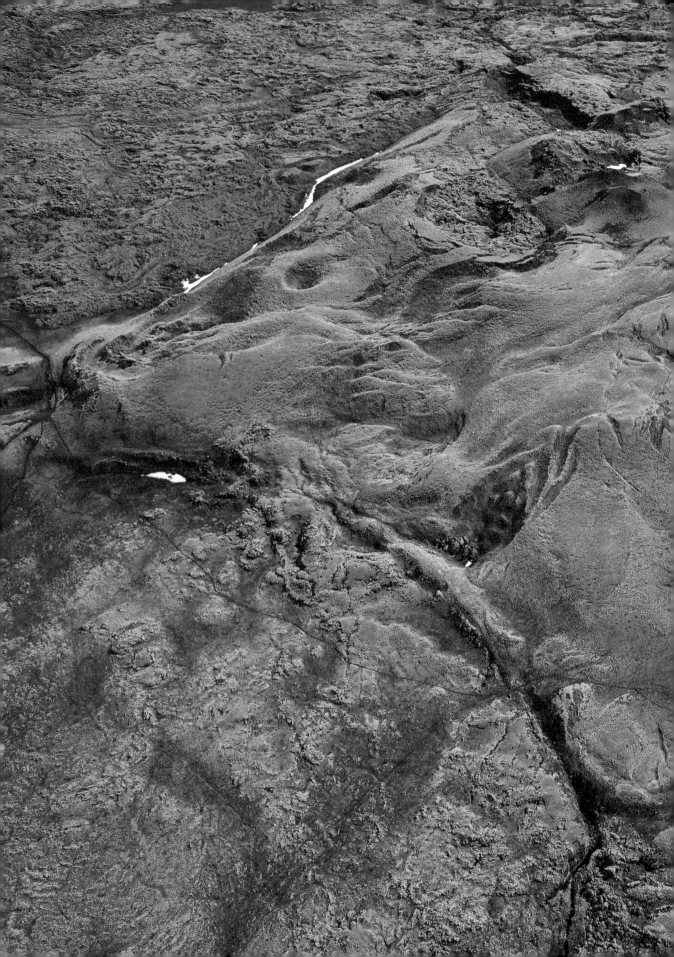

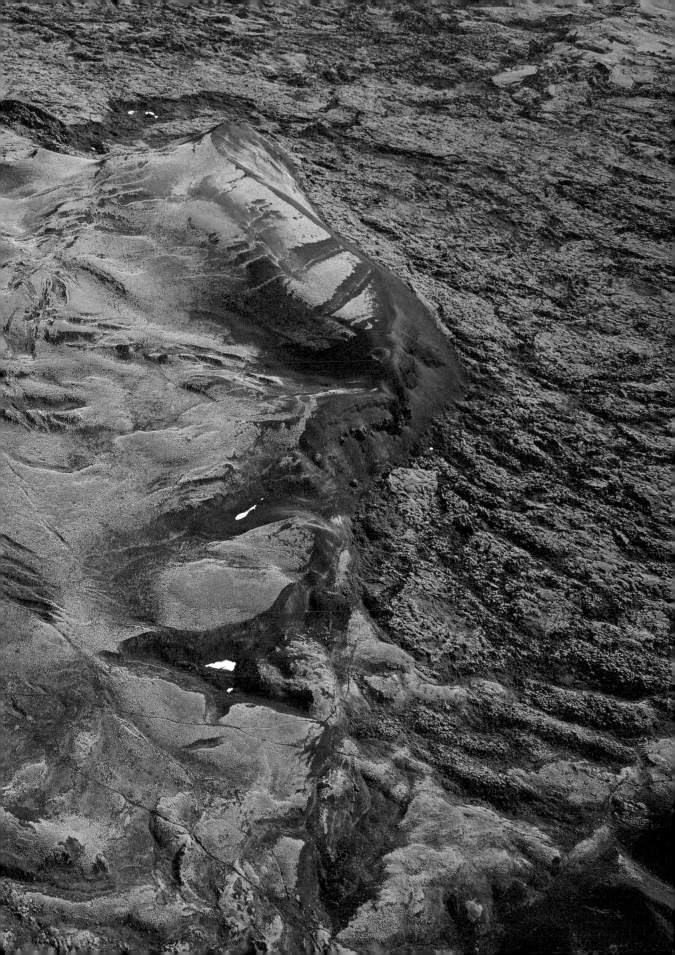

Table 6.2 Essential Minerals and What They Do

Mineral	Sources	Function in the Body	DRI (adult)*	Estimated Macrobiotic Diet Value†
Calcium	Daikon radish Dandelion greens Dulse Kale Kelp Leafy greens Nuts Parsley Sea vegetables Sesame seeds Soy foods Watercress	Builds healthy bones and teeth. Helps blood to clot. Regulates heartbeat and mineral balance.	1,300 mg	1,350 mg
Chlorine	Celery Green cabbage Kale Lettuce Parsnips Radishes Sea vegetables Vegetables	Aids digestion and elimination. Sustains normal heart activity.	Trace	Trace
Iodine	Fish Leafy greens Sea vegetables Vegetables (organically grown)	Stimulates the thyroid gland, which regulates the rate of digestion. Important for growth and development.	150 mcg	150–300 mcg
Iron	Beans and legumes Fruits (dried and fresh) Kelp Leafy greens Nuts Sea vegetables Seeds Tekka Whole grains	Helps to form hemo-globin and myoglobin. Aids oxygen transport to cells and prevents anemia.	18 mg	39.3 mg

Mineral	Sources	Function in the Body	DRI (adult)*	Estimated Macrobiotic Diet Value†
Phosphorus	Beans and legumes Fruits Nuts Pumpkin and squash seeds Sea vegetables Sesame seeds Sunflower seeds Vegetables Whole grains	Builds and maintains bones, teeth, hair, and nervous tissue. Assists cells in absorbing fats and carbohydrates.	1,250 mg	1,539 mg
Potassium	Beans and legumes Cabbage Chestnuts Dulse Fruits (fresh and dried) Kelp Leafy greens Nuts Vegetables	Maintains mineral balance and weight. Tones muscles.	—	3,666 mg
Sodium	Cucumbers Horseradish Leafy greens Miso Root vegetables Sea vegetables Sesame seeds Tamari	Aids digestion, speeds elimination of carbon dioxide, and regulates body fluids and heart action.	500 mg	2,560 mg

Sources: *DRIs: The figures used are adapted from the DRIs established for adults by the Food and Nutrition Board of the U.S. National Institute of Medicine, 2001.

†Estimated nutritional content of the macrobiotic diet (for one person, for one day) is based on *USDA Composition of Foods Handbook No. 8.*

Abbreviations used in the above table:

IU: international units (a measure of activity, not weight)

mg: milligrams (a measure of weight)

mcg: micrograms (a measure of weight equal to 1/1000 milligram)

Note: A dash signifies that no DRI has been established.

Olafur Eliasson
Lava kaleidoscope, 2012

The workshop How to Train Compassion was hosted July 20–23 , 2011, at Studio Olafur Eliasson and organized by Tania Singer, professor of neuroscience and director of the Department of Social Neuroscience at the Max Planck Institute, Leipzig. The workshop brought together scientists researching compassion, clinical psychologists, and contemplative scholars to explore how secular compassion-training programs could serve science and society today. In addition to presentations and panel discussions, the event featured compassion exercises and meditation sessions led by Buddhist masters within the artist's studio. Cooking and eating were emphasized as forms of meditation to complement each day's topic. The vegetarian and vegan dishes prepared by Lauren Maurer and Asako Iwama invited the participants to become aware of their bodies' sensations and to explore how we are connected to the universe through air, water, and soil. After the event, Tania Singer and psychologist Matthias Bolz compiled documentation of the workshop and contributions from many of the participants into the e-book *Compassion: Bridging Practice and Science*. The film *Raising Compassion,* produced by Studio Olafur Eliasson, presents a round of conversations sparked by the workshop.

VII   Minerals

For years, I have been interested in how we make the feeling of being connected to other people – of being fundamentally interdependent – felt. It's crucial to understand the greater cause-and-effect relations, our impact on the world and its impact on us. This is exactly the moment where you begin to ask: How do I feel in a group? What is collectivity? What is my notion of community and how do I experience being part of it? When does one begin to feel responsibility toward somebody else? Somebody next to you, somebody in another room, or in another country? In 2010, I met Tania Singer, who introduced the concept of compassion as a vital new field for scientific research. I was really excited to see how her research offered another language for talking about connectivity. As a bridge-builder, she boldly connects people in her research, not shying away from areas such as spirituality and contemplative practices. As an artist, I find that fundamental inclusivity very inspiring. There's no doubt that compassion is a concept for the twenty-first century.

Olafur Eliasson

The recipes collected on the following pages present some of the studio's vegan dishes. These were prepared during the Compassion Seminar to cater to the dietary needs of many of the seminar's participants.

Cooking Brown Rice   Serves 6 | 60

In a pressure cooker

14 oz (400 g) | 9 lb (4 kg) . . . . brown rice
a pinch of . . . . salt

Rinse and thoroughly drain the rice. Place rice in the pressure cooker (pot), add 2 cups (500 ml) or 5 quarts (5 liters) water, and a pinch of salt, close the lid firmly, and bring to a boil over medium heat until the pressure level has been reached. Reduce heat to low and cook for 40 minutes. Remove the pressure cooker from the heat (keep the lid on) and let steam for 20 minutes. Cooking whole-grain rice in a pressure cooker brings a crisp flavor and sticky consistency to the grain.

Note
If you have an additional small ceramic or metal cooker with a lid that can fit inside the pressure cooker, try this variation: Place the rice, water, and salt in the smaller pot. Pour 3 cups (750 ml) water into the pressure cooker; place the small pot with lid into the pressure cooker, close firmly, and cook according to instructions. This technique produces an even stronger flavor.

Without a pressure cooker

14 oz (400 g) | 9 lb (4 kg) . . . . brown rice
a pinch of . . . . salt

Rinse the brown rice and drain well. Place the rice, 3⅓ cups (800 ml) or 2 gallons (8 liters) water, and salt into a heavy-bottom pot with a tight-fitting lid. Bring to a boil over medium heat. Cover, reduce heat to its lowest setting, and cook, uninterrupted, for 30 minutes. Peek inside to make sure the water has been completely absorbed. If not, cook a bit longer. If the rice is too dry, add a bit more water. Turn off heat and allow it to steam an additional 10 minutes.

(Soaking the rice in the water for 1 hour before cooking will create a stickier and more tender consistency.)

Vegetable Consommé   Makes about 7 quarts (7 liters)

Adapted from *Inochi no soup* (Soup of Life)

1 lb 2 oz (500 g)	potatoes, sliced
5 oz (150 g)	onions, sliced
4½ oz (150 g)	carrots, sliced
4½ oz (150 g)	celery, sliced
1 tsp	sea salt
4 strips	kombu or wakame
2	ume seeds
4	dried shiitake
10	white peppercorns
2	bay leaves

Place all vegetables into a heavy-bottom pot and cover with 7 quarts (7 liters) water. Add the salt, kombu, ume seeds, dried shiitake, peppercorns, and bay leaves, and bring to a boil over medium heat. Decrease heat to low and cook for 20 minutes. Remove the kombu and cook 20 minutes more. During this time the taste might change a lot, so taste often and, when you find it to be right, turn off the heat. Immediately drain the stock, removing any vegetables. Taste and adjust seasonings if necessary.

This consommé can be served as is or ladled over brown rice and sprinkled with toasted sesame seeds and nori strips. It can also be frozen for later use.

Tofu Balls with Cilantro and Sesame   Serves 6 | 60

1 lb 2 oz (500 g) | 11 lb (5 kg)	firm tofu
5 oz (150 g) | 1.5 kg	rice flour, plus extra as needed
2 TB | 7 oz (200 g)	potato or corn starch
1 TB | ⅔ cup (150 ml)	soy sauce
1 TB | ⅔ cup (150 ml)	mirin or sake
1 thumb- | 2 hand-size pieces	ginger, finely grated
1 | 5 bunch/es	cilantro (coriander), finely chopped
1 TB | 5 oz (150 g)	sesame seeds, roasted
	flour for coating
	oil for frying

Drain the tofu very well and place a plate and a weight on top for 30 minutes to release any remaining liquid. Dry well. Place the rice flour, starch, soy sauce, mirin, and ginger in a food processor and blend. Add the cilantro and sesame seeds and mix. Form 2-inch (5 cm) balls and gently press them to a thickness of about 1 inch (2 cm). If necessary, add more rice flour to get the right consistency. Coat the tofu balls in flour.

In a heavy-bottom saucepan, pour oil to a depth of at least 2¾ inches (7 cm) and heat to 350°F/180°C. Carefully slide the tofu balls, a few at a time, into the hot oil. Fry until they are cooked on the inside and golden brown on the outside, turning with a slotted spoon when necessary. Transfer to paper towels to drain and serve immediately, or keep warm, uncovered, in a preheated 200°F/100°C/Gas Mark 1/2 oven for up to 30 minutes. Repeat the process for the remaining balls.

Eat as burgers with a bit of grated ginger on top, alone with soy sauce, or as a soup with hot kombu-shiitake stock or Vegetable Consommé (see above).

Azuki Bean Paste   Makes about 3 cups (750 ml)

7 oz (200 g) . . . . azuki beans, washed
3½ oz (100 g) . . . . black sugar (or muscovado),
                              plus extra as needed
1 tsp . . . . salt, plus extra as needed

In a pot, cover the beans with 2½ cups (600 ml) cold water and cook about 60 to 90 minutes, or until tender, adding water as necessary to keep the beans just covered. Drain, reserving the cooking water. Add sugar and season with salt, and cook for 10 more minutes, taking care not to let the pot burn. Taste and adjust the salt and sugar as necessary. Once done, blend the beans with an immersion blender or food processor, adding in the reserved water to reach the desired consistency. Let cool and eat as dessert.

(The paste is delicious when served with whipped cream, mascarpone, or crème fraîche, and topped with Soy Milk Jelly with Black Sugar Syrup [see below] and strawberries.)

Soy Milk Jelly with Black Sugar Syrup   Serves 6 | 60

2½ cups (600 ml) |
    6 quarts (6 liters) . . . . . . soy milk (or almond, oat,
                                    or rice milk)
3 g | 1 oz (30 g) . . . . agar-agar
3½ oz (100 g) | 2¼ lb (1 kg) . . black sugar
2 TB | 300 ml . . . . honey

To make the jelly, place the milk and agar-agar into a pot and bring to a boil. Once the agar-agar has dissolved, pour the mixture into a container, let cool, and refrigerate until set.

To prepare the syrup, place the black sugar and ¼ cup (50 ml) or 2 cups (500 ml) water in a heavy-bottom saucepan over medium heat and simmer until the sugar dissolves. Stir in the honey and let cool. The syrup can be refrigerated for up to 3 weeks.

When the jelly has set, cut into diamonds and serve with the syrup. It pairs nicely with diced mango, melon, or banana. Alternatively serve with Azuki Bean Paste (see above), Puréed Apricot with Vanilla Beans (see page 234), or ice cream.

Mixed Rice
see page 150

Chinese Clear Egg Soup Serves 6 | 60

6¼ cups	4 gallons (15 liters)	Kombu Stock (see below)
3½ TB	2 cups (500 ml)	sake
1 thumb-	1 hand-size piece	ginger, cut into matchsticks
3	30	eggs
1 TB	3½ oz (100 g)	corn starch (cornflour), optional, to thicken
3½ oz (100 g)	2¼ lb (1 kg)	heirloom corn kernels
1 tsp	¼ cup (50 ml)	soy sauce
	freshly ground black pepper
2	20 stems	scallions (spring onions), finely chopped
1 TB	5 oz (150 g)	sesame seeds, toasted
	toasted sesame oil

In a heavy-bottom saucepan, bring the stock, sake, and ginger to a boil. While the stock boils, whisk the eggs in a small bowl. In another small bowl, mix the corn starch and a bit of cold water into a paste. Add to the stock and return the liquid to a boil. After a couple of minutes, while stirring the stock, slowly add the eggs in a circular motion, making sure to disperse them evenly across the surface. Add the corn, soy sauce, and pepper. Sprinkle in the scallions and sesame seeds, and drizzle with sesame oil. Serve immediately.

Kombu Stock Makes 2 quarts (2 liters)

4 strips	dried kombu (2×8 in/5×20 cm)

It is sometimes difficult to find kombu (kelp) in Europe, and, if necessary, it can easily be substituted with wakame from an organic shop. Soak the kombu in 2 quarts (2 liters) water overnight. In the morning, the soaking water can be used for stock: it will have already absorbed flavor and minerals from the kombu. Alternatively, if you want a more intense flavor, transfer the kombu with its soaking water to a pot and cook over a very low heat, making sure to remove the kombu shortly before the water comes to a boil. This will ensure that the soup stock remains clear. Reserve the kombu in a small bowl for later use.

Wakame Salad Serves 6 | 60

50	1 lb 2 oz (500 g)	wakame
1	10	cucumbers, thinly sliced
1 pinch	1 tsp	salt
½	5 tsp	sugar
1 TB	⅔ cup (150 ml)	apple cider vinegar
1 TB	⅔ cup (150 ml)	roasted sesame oil
1 TB	5 oz (150 g)	sesame seeds, toasted

Soak the wakame in water for 10 minutes. Drain and chop into 2-inch (5 cm) pieces. Blanch the wakame briefly in boiling water. Drain and transfer to a bowl of ice water for a few seconds before draining again very well. Sprinkle the cucumber with salt. Let sit for 5 minutes and press dry. In a small bowl, toss the wakame with the cucumber, sugar, vinegar, sesame oil, and sesame seeds and toss to combine.

Although always wrapped up in a sheet of nori, these rice balls can contain a variety of fillings, such as Umeboshi (see page 241), pickled seaweed, tempura, or salmon. Conventional Japanese wisdom says that the deliciousness of the rice ball depends on the palm that made it. Rice balls are a comfort food, something to be eaten even when one is too tired to chew.

Mixed Brown and Black Rice Balls	Makes 12 | 120 balls

4 | 40 sheets	nori
1 lb 2 oz (500 g) | 11 lb (5 kg) . .	brown rice
3½ oz (100 g) | 2¼ lb (1 kg) . .	black rice
. . . .	salt
1¾ oz (50 g) | 1 lb 2 oz (500 g) .	Miso (see page 221)
1 thumb- | 1 hand-size piece .	ginger, very finely grated
3½ oz (100 g) | 2 lb 3 oz (1 kg) .	sesame seeds, toasted and ground roughly

Cut the nori sheets lengthwise into quarters and put aside, taking care to keep them dry. Separately, rinse the brown and black rice and drain well. Place in a pressure cooker (pot) with 6¾ cups (1.5 liters) or 4 gallons (15 liters) water with a generous pinch of salt. Close the lid firmly and bring to a boil over medium heat until the pressure level is reached. Decrease heat to low and cook for 40 minutes. Remove the pressure cooker from heat (keep the lid on) and let steam until ready for use.

While the rice is cooking, prepare the filling for the rice balls. Combine the miso paste, ginger, and one third of the sesame seeds and mix. Prepare your workspace or a table with a bowl of cold water, a small bowl of salt, the miso filling, and a shallow bowl filled with the remaining ground sesame seeds.

To make the rice balls, first wet your hands with a little water and rub a touch of salt between them. Take a handful of rice and form it into a ball. Make an indentation in it, fill it with the miso mixture, and then close it. Pass the rice ball gently from hand to hand, being careful not to put too much pressure on it. The shape of your hands will mold the sides of the rice balls into triangles as you work.

Gently dip the rice balls into the roasted sesame seeds, covering them evenly on all sides, and set aside. Serve with the dried nori seaweed on the side, using it to wrap the rice balls and eat by hand.

Serve with Miso Soup and Seaweed and Cucumber Salad (see page 325).

Miso Soup   Serves 6 | 60

¾ oz (20 g) | 7 oz (200 g) . . .	wakame
1 | 8	daikon radishes, cut into matchsticks
2 medium | 4½ lb (2 kg)	carrots, cut into matchsticks
300 g | 6 lb 11 oz (3 kg)	tofu, diced
5 TB | 1⅔ lb (750 g)	Miso (see page 221)
1 TB | ⅔ cup (150 ml)	tahini

Soak the wakame for 20 minutes in 2 quarts or 2 gallons cold water. Remove from the water (which will be used as the stock), cut into 1-inch (2 cm) strips, and set aside. Bring the stock to a boil, adding the daikon and the carrots. Once the vegetables have cooked, add the tofu.

Ladle 2 spoonfuls of the wakame stock into a separate bowl, mix in miso and tahini until dissolved, and set aside. Add the wakame strips to the remaining stock and bring to a boil. Remove from heat and add the miso mixture. At this point, the soup should not come to a boil again, as this destroys not only the flavor but also miso's live cultures.

Note
Traditionally, this soup is made with kombu stock, although kombu can often be difficult to find in Europe. To try this variation, leave out the wakame and instead use the Kombu Stock on page 321.

Seaweed and Cucumber Salad   Serves 6 | 60

1¾ oz (50 g) | 1 lb 2 oz (500 g) . .	hijiki or other seaweed, soaked for 20 minutes and drained
1 | 10	cucumbers
1 tsp | 3 TB	Umeboshi (see page 241), chopped
1 | 8	cloves garlic, ground
½ | 5	lemon/s, juiced and zested
. . . .	salt and freshly ground black pepper
1 TB | ⅔ cup (150 ml)	olive oil, plus extra as needed
1 small | 1 kg	red onion, thinly sliced
1 TB | 5 oz (150 g)	sesame seeds, toasted

Chop the seaweed into 2-inch (5 cm) pieces. Blanch it briefly in boiling water, drain, transfer to a bowl with ice water for a few seconds, and then drain again.

Quarter the cucumbers lengthwise; halve each section again lengthwise, ending up with 8 long pieces. In a small bowl, combine the umeboshi, garlic, lemon juice and zest, salt, pepper, and olive oil. Add the seaweed, cucumber, red onion, and sesame seeds and toss to combine.

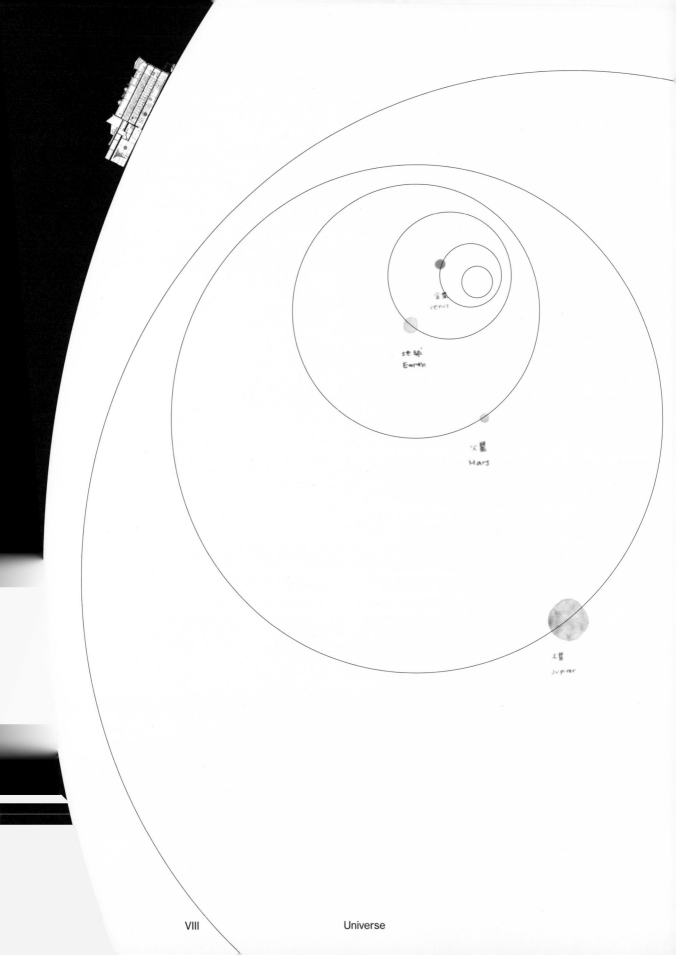

金星
venus

地球
Earth

火星
Mars

木星
Jupiter

土星
Saturn

Universe

Asako Iwama and
Lauren Maurer

"In every apple you are eating Jupiter; in every plum, Saturn." Rudolf Steiner, in his thinking about biodynamic agriculture, theorized that the connection between food and the universe is an exchange of energy, and that plants and their fruit are the result of cosmic forces. Physicists and biologists would agree that apples and plums only come into being through the energy of one celestial body: the light of the sun.

At the studio, our interest in biodynamic principles deepened as the result of a personal encounter. We first saw and tasted produce from a local biodynamic farm at the organic farmer's market on Chamissoplatz in Berlin. The small tomatoes from the farm, called Apfeltraum, were dense and tasty; their green beans and cilantro (coriander), the freshest around. Apfeltraum made us realize we could cook with biodynamically farmed, local produce in the studio too. Anne and Boris, from Apfeltraum, came to visit us, and we paid a visit to their farm collective near the village of Eggersdorf, Germany. Apfeltraum operates according to the standards of the Demeter association, which calls for holistic biodynamic farming methods, such as using dung from the cows that are kept by the farm as natural fertilizer. To us, one of the strengths of biodynamic farming is how much it draws on

inherited knowledge — from both nature and people. The overall approach aims rather at giving back to nature than taking from it. This is why beekeeping plays such an important role at Apfeltraum. Since most plants depend on bees for pollination, the threat of bee population decline (likely linked to pollution and pesticides, among other things) is a threat to plant life and therefore to all life that depends on plants. Over the years, the produce of biodynamic farming and beekeeping — freshly harvested, seasonal greens for our salads and honey for the occasional studio breakfast — have become staples of our daily routine.

We often wonder how it can be that we feel so disconnected from the life cycles we are clearly part of, why we have lost the awareness of sharing a planet and ultimately a universe. Our planet's orbit around the sun gives us solstices and equinoxes, defines day and night and seasons. It determines climate and weather, creates distinct habitats, flora, and fauna. The moon moves the enormous water masses that cover vast surfaces of the earth, its tidal force a visible effect of gravity. Ultimately, the origin of life goes back to one big initial explosion of stars. Today, we still are made up of the same basic chemical elements that led to this explosion: We are particles of stars.

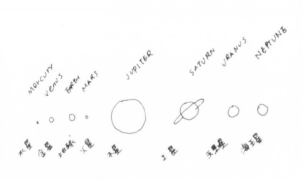

MERCURY VENUS EARTH MARS JUPITER SATURN URANUS NEPTUNE

水星 金星 地球 火星 木星 土星 天王星 海王星

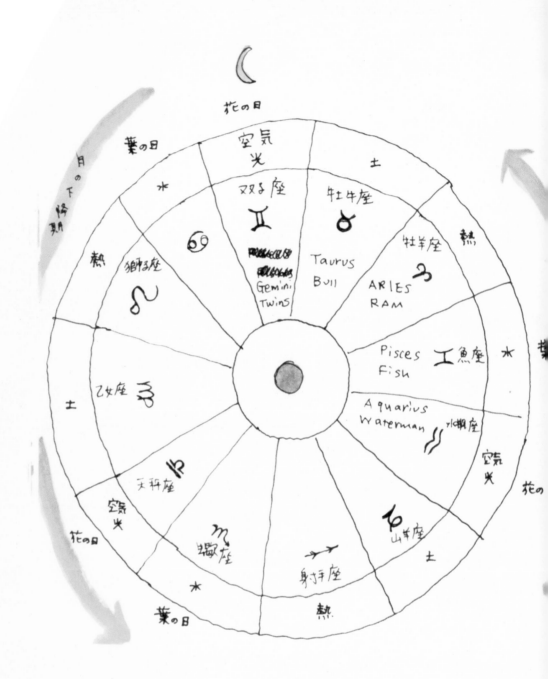

Olafur Eliasson
Orbital life, 2010

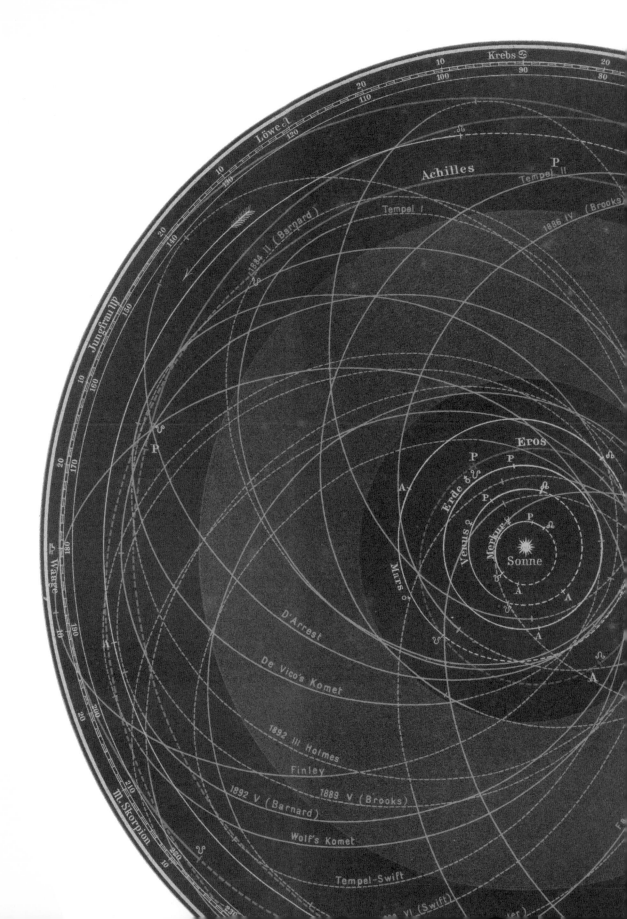

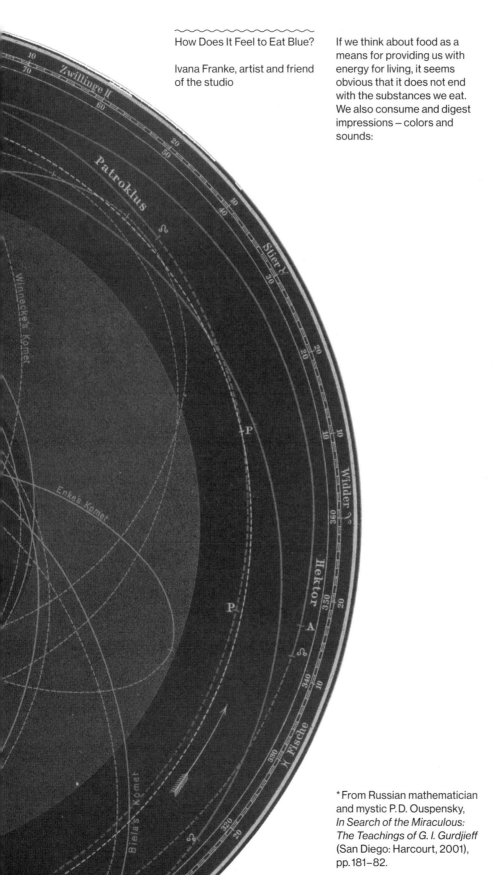

How Does It Feel to Eat Blue?

Ivana Franke, artist and friend of the studio

If we think about food as a means for providing us with energy for living, it seems obvious that it does not end with the substances we eat. We also consume and digest impressions – colors and sounds:

"The human organism receives three kinds of food:
1. The ordinary food we eat
2. The air we breathe
3. Our impressions
It is not difficult to agree that air is a kind of food for the organism. But in what way impressions can be food may appear at first difficult to understand. We must however remember that, with every external impression, whether it takes the form of sound, or vision, or smell, we receive from outside a certain amount of energy, a certain number of vibrations, this energy which enters the organism from outside is food ... If the flow of impressions were to be stopped in some way or if the organism were deprived of its capacity for receiving impressions, it would immediately die. The flow of impressions coming to us from outside is like a driving belt communicating motion to us. The principal motor for us is nature, the surrounding world. Nature transmits to us through our impressions the energy by which we live and move and have our being. If the inflow of this energy is arrested, our machine will immediately stop working. Thus, of the three kinds of food, the most important for us is impressions." *

In this sense, an artist's studio as a whole could be thought of as a kitchen – for cooking impressions and providing humans with a particular kind of food. The tastes of spaces and colours that come from Olafur's kitchen feel like an influx of energy driving us to embark upon a cosmic flight in our minds.

* From Russian mathematician and mystic P. D. Ouspensky, *In Search of the Miraculous: The Teachings of G. I. Gurdjieff* (San Diego: Harcourt, 2001), pp. 181–82.

Asako Iwama and
Lauren Maurer visiting the
Apfeltraum farm, 2008

On July 16, 2010, the opening of *On Eating,* at Grey Sheep, was a communal harvest celebration. Fresh greens, herbs, and flowers from the studio garden were dipped into batter, fried, and served as tempura. The exhibition communicated how everything, from soil and the microbes in the soil to seeds and plants, is connected to the sun, the moon, and the universe. The concrete floor of the project space was covered with soil: visitors entering and leaving the room carried bits of soil across the threshold onto the cobbled stones outside. A microscope was set up so that guests could see microorganisms in motion. The worm compost bin could also be observed. Texts and books on topics as diverse as composting, gene modification, and the ownership of water were presented on specially built shelves. Chalk drawings of the lunar calendar on the floor and models of the solar system visualized constellations and the arrangement of planets and alluded to biodynamic principles of farming, which relate to cosmic forces.

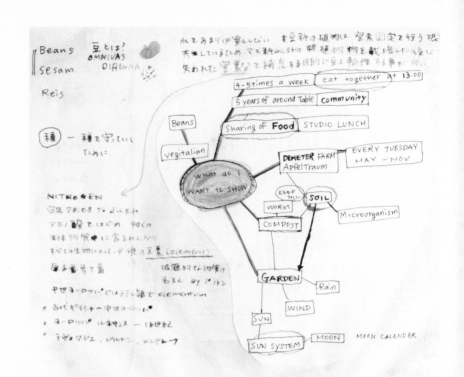

Grey Sheep: On Eating

For us, the opening and exhibition at Grey Sheep allowed us to share with the studio and beyond – for the first time – the different ideas flowing into our everyday cooking. We were thinking about plants and how water and nutrients enter and travel through them, about microorganisms, worms, and composting – so we dedicated the exhibition space to microorganisms and our awareness of them. We prepared green plants from the roof for the event: We made tempura from carrot tops and fennel greens, sage and cilantro (coriander), and pumpkin and zucchini flowers. From arugula (rocket) we created fresh falafel. Around this time, we also started thinking about eating on the atomic level and about molecules. We became interested in biodynamic agriculture, farming practices informed by Rudolf Steiner's thinking on the interrelation of food growth and planetary forces. We reflected on the lunar calendar and planting according to it, thinking about the soil and its microorganisms and their relation to the moon cycle and zodiac. We also thought about orbital life, so we showed an antique orrery alongside a planetary model by Olafur, in which a lemon replaced the sun for the duration of the show. The window next to the kitchen was used to present information on topics such as the quality of soil and how it is related to traditional knowledge, and on agriculture and the biodynamic farm Apfeltraum. We shared texts by Vandana Shiva about her seed bank project, her activism against gene-modified foods and the commodification of seeds. Books and texts, food and soil, planetary models and drawings reflected ideas that continue to move and inspire us.

Asako Iwama and
Lauren Maurer

The tempura we made for the opening of *Grey Sheep: On Eating* used ingredients sourced exclusively from the rooftop garden. This meant that we had to be a bit more open-minded and experimental about what we prepared, simply to have enough to go around. Herbs and flowers are not normally found in tempura dishes, but they actually work very well!

Flower and Herb Tempura

7 oz (200 g)	all-purpose flour
1	egg
a variety of	flowers and herbs, including zucchini flowers, pumpkin flowers, elderberry flowers, sage, fennel, and dill
	sesame or vegetable oil for frying

Sift the flour to allow it to aerate. Whisk together the egg with a generous ¾ cup (200 ml) ice water. Pour the egg mixture into the flour and mix until just lightly blended. Do not over-mix or allow the batter to become too sticky. This will ensure a crispy tempura.

In a heavy-bottom saucepan, pour the oil to a depth of at least 2¾ inches (7 cm) and heat to around 350°F/185°C/Gas Mark 4. Dip 6 flowers or herb sprigs into the batter, and, one at a time, slip them into the hot oil. Fry until they are tender and golden brown, turning as neces-sary with a slotted spoon. When done, transfer the tempura to paper towels to drain. Serve immediately or keep warm, uncovered, in a preheated 200°F/100°C/Gas Mark 1/2 oven for up to 30 minutes. Repeat this process with the remaining flowers and herbs. Serve with Tentsuyu Sauce (see below).

This batter can also be used to fry a more standard selection of cubed or thinly sliced vege-tables, such as zucchini, carrots, potatoes, peppers, eggplant (aubergine), pumpkin, onion, corn, asparagus, and radicchio.

Tentsuyu Sauce   Makes 1¼ cups (300 ml)

2 pieces	kombu
scant ¼ cup (50 ml)	soy sauce
scant ¼ cup (50 ml)	mirin
3 TB	daikon, grated
1 TB	fresh ginger, grated

Soak the kombu in ¾ cup (200ml) water for 30 minutes. Transfer the kombu and water to a pot and bring to a boil. Remove from heat, strain out and discard kombu, and add the soy sauce and mirin. Bring to a boil again. Add the grated daikon and ginger and serve.

Carrot and Radicchio Garden Salad   Serves 6 | 60

By Thórdís Magnea Jónsdóttir

2 TB | 1¼ cup (300 ml)	sherry vinegar or lemon juice
1 tsp | 3 TB	honey
½ tsp | 1 TB	dijon mustard
½ tsp | 1½ TB	sea salt
2 TB | 1¼ cup (300 ml)	olive oil
1 lb 2 oz (500 g) | 11 lb (5 kg) . .	carrots, roughly grated
½ | 5 medium head/s	radicchio, finely chopped
2 sprigs | 1 bunch	parsley, finely chopped
2 TB | 14 oz (400 g)	capers
. . . .	freshly ground black pepper
2 TB | 7 oz (200 g)	sunflower seeds, roasted
. . . .	sundried tomatoes (optional)
. . . .	black olives (optional)

Combine the sherry vinegar, honey, dijon mustard, salt, and olive oil and set aside. Mix the carrots, radicchio, parsley, and capers in a large bowl. Add the dressing and pepper and thoroughly mix with your hands. Toss with the sunflower seeds and serve. You can also serve this salad with sundried tomatoes and black olives.

Green Salad with Balsamic Dijon Dressing   Serves 6 | 60

3 TB | 1¾ cups (450 ml)	white balsamic vinegar
3 TB | 1¾ cups (450 ml)	fresh lemon juice
1 tsp | 3 TB	honey
1 tsp | 3 TB	dijon mustard
½ | 4 clove/s.	garlic, minced
. . . .	salt and freshly ground black pepper
3 TB | 1¾ cups (450 ml)	olive oil
1 | 8 head/s	lettuce, chopped

Combine the vinegar, lemon juice, honey, mustard, garlic, salt, and pepper and then slowly whisk in the olive oil. Pour the dressing over lettuce and toss to combine.

Tomato Secco

2¼ lb (1 kg)	tomatoes, halved
6	garlic cloves, finely sliced
. . . . . , ...	coarse sea salt
. . . .	extra-virgin olive oil

Preheat the oven to 200°F/ 100°C/Gas Mark 1/2. Set the tomatoes on a parchment-lined baking sheet (tray), cut side up. Sprinkle with garlic, sea salt, and olive oil, and slow-roast in the oven for 3 hours. Alternatively, the tomatoes can be dried by placing them in the sun for up to 2 days, bringing them inside at night.

"It is believed that the universe we live in began as a ball of fire. This ball of fire caused a tremendous explosion about fifteen billion years ago.

The ball of fire swelled so rapidly that it reached the size of the current solar system after a ten to the power of sixth of a second. By then, protons, neutrons and mesons that compose the nucleus of an atom already existed in the universe.

Seven hundred thousand years after the explosion, nuclei joined with electrons to form atoms. The first stars appeared after four billion years and the solar system was born after ten billion years … When a star… explodes, it causes hydrogen, carbon, oxygen, and helium to fly off into all directions of the universe as interstellar matter, becoming buds of new stars to be formed over time.

The Earth we live in, too, was born around 4.6 billion years ago out of such interstellar matter. It is believed that lightning and ultraviolet light affected the hydrogen, oxygen, carbon and nitrogen on earth to join together and split apart over time, eventually giving rise, by accident, to molecules that form the basis of life.

We are made of particles of stars."

‖ Keiko Yanagisawa ‖
‖ *Inochi to hoshyanou* ‖
‖ (Life and Radiation) ‖

Olafur Eliasson
Icelandic tellurium, 2008

Works Cited

Aihara, Herman. "The Spiralic Concept of Man." In George Ohsawa. *The Order of the Universe*. Chico, California: George Ohsawa Macrobiotic Foundation, 1986.

Appelhof, Mary. *Worms Eat My Garbage: How to Set Up and Maintain a Worm Composting System*. Kalamazoo, Michigan: Flower Press, 1982.

Carrarini, Rose. *Breakfast, Lunch, Tea: Rose Bakery*. New York: Phaidon, 2006.

Carroll, John Phillip. *Pies and Tarts*. Ed. Chuck Williams. San Francisco: Weldon Owen, 1992.

Clark, Samantha, and Samuel Clark. *Moro East*. London: Ebury, 2007.

"Composition of the Human Body." *Wikipedia: The Free Encyclopedia*. Web. 24 Oct. 2013.

Devi, Yamuna. *The Vegetarian Table: India*. San Francisco: Chronicle Books, 1997.

Gray, Rose, and Ruth Rogers. *The River Cafe Cookbook*. London: Ebury, 1995.

Gray, Rose, and Ruth Rogers. *River Cafe Cook Book Two*. London: Ebury, 1997.

Howard, Albert. *The Soil and Health: A Study of Organic Agriculture*. Lexington: The University Press of Kentucky, 2007.

Katz, Sandor Ellix. *The Art of Fermentation: An In-Depth Exploration of Essential Concepts and Processes from Around the World*. White River Junction, Vermont: Chelsea Green Publishing, 2012.

Katzen, Molly. *The New Moosewood Cookbook*. Berkeley: Ten Speed, 2000.

Kushi, Michio, with Stephen Blauer. *The Macrobiotic Way: The Complete Macrobiotic Lifestyle Book*. New York: Penguin, 2004.

McGee, Harold. *On Food and Cooking: The Science and Lore of the Kitchen*. New York: Scribner, 1984/2004.

Ohsawa, Lima. *Macrobiotic Cuisine*. Tokyo: Japan Publications, 1984.

Ottolenghi, Yotam, and Sami Tamimi. *Jerusalem: A Cookbook*. Berkeley: Ten Speed, 2012.

Rosengarten, David, with Joel Dean and Giorgio DeLuca. *The Dean and DeLuca Cookbook*. New York: Random House, 1996.

Shiva, Vandana. *Annadāna: The Gift of Food*. New Dehli: Navdanya, [No Year].

Shiva, Vandana. *Seed Dictatorship and Food Fascism*. New Delhi: Navdanya, [No Year].

Smith, Delia. *Delia's How to Cook, Book Three*. London: BBC Worldwide, 2001.

Steiner, Rudolf. *Spiritual Foundations for the Renewal of Agriculture – A Course of Lectures Held at Koberwitz, Silesia, June 7 to June 16, 1924*. Junction City, Oregon: Bio-Dynamic Farming and Gardening Association, 1993.

Tanaka, Reiko. *Honkide oyatsu* (Serious Snacks). Tokyo: Bunka Shuppankyoku, 2002.

Tatsumi, Yoshiko. "Diet and Life: For Humans to Become People." Unpublished interview with Fukuoka Shin-Ichi. Trans. Asako Iwama.

Tatsumi, Yoshiko. *Anata no tameni: inochi wo sasaeru soup* (Soup of Life). Tokyo: Chikuma-Syobo, 2002.

Varona, Verne. "A Guide to the Macrobiotic Principles." *Macrobiotic Guide*. Web. 5 Nov. 2013.

Waters, Alice. *The Art of Simple Food: Notes, Lessons, and Recipes from a Delicious Revolution*. New York: Clarkson Potter, 2007.

Yanagisawa, Keiko. *Inochi to hoshyanou* (Life and Radiation). Trans. Naoki Matsuyuma. Tokyo: Chikuma-Syobo, 2007.

Further Reading

Abehsera, Michel. *Zen Macrobiotic Cooking: A Book of Oriental and Traditional Recipes*. New York: Citadel, 2001.

Atlas der Globalisierung: Die Welt von morgen. Ed. Barbara Bauer. Berlin: Taz, 2012.

Bertolli, Paul, with Alice Waters. *Chez Parnisse Cooking*. New York: Random House, 1994.

Bittman, Mark. *How to Cook Everything Vegetarian: Simple Meatless Recipes for Great Food*. Hoboken, New Jersey: Wiley, 2007.

Black Gold. Dir. Nick and Marc Francis. Speakit, 2006. Film.

Caroll, Sean B., Jennifer K. Grenier, and Scott D. Weatherbee. *From DNA to Diversity: Molecular Genetics and the Evolution of Animal Design*. Maldon, Massachusetts: Blackwell, 2001.

Coles, Alex. "Studio Olafur Eliasson." *The Transdisciplinary Studio*. Berlin: Sternberg Press, 2012.

Compassion: Bridging Practice and Science. Ed. Tania Singer and Matthias Bolz. eBook / Web. 5 Nov. 2013.

Darwin, Charles. *The Works of Charles Darwin, Volume 28: The Formation of Vegetable Mold Through the Action of Worms with Observations on Their Habits*. New York: New York University, 2010.

Fukuoka, Masanobu. *The One-Straw Revolution: An Introduction to Natural Farming*. New York: New York Review Books, 2009.

"Gandhji and Diet." *Gandhi Research Foundation*. 5 Nov. 2013. Web.

Goethe, Johann Wolfgang von. *The Metamorphosis of Plants.* Trans. Douglas Miller. Boston: MIT, 2009.

Gray, Rose, and Ruth Rogers. *River Cafe Cook Book Green.* London: Ebury, 2001.

Heistinger, Andrea, and Arche Noah. *Bio-Gemüse: Sortenvielfalt für den eigenen Garten.* Stuttgart: Löwenzahn, 2010.

Jones, Caroline. "The Server / User Mode." *Artforum International* (October 2007): 316–25.

Katz, Sandor Ellix. *Wild Fermentation: The Flavor, Nutrition, and Craft of Live-Culture Foods.* White River Junction, Vermont: Chelsea Green Publishing, 2003.

Kushi, Michio, and Alex Jack: *The Macrobiotic Path to Total Health: A Complete Guide to Naturally Preventing and Relieving More than 200 Chronic Conditions and Disorders.* New York: Ballantine, 2003.

Life in Space 3: 09.05.2008. Ed. Olafur Eliasson, Andreas Koch, Anna Engberg-Pedersen, Camilla Kragelund / Studio Olafur Eliasson; Dietmar Graber, Christian Hogenmüller, Astrid Kühn-Ulrich. Dornbirn: Zumtobel, 2008.

Life Is Space 4. Ed. Olafur Eliasson, Anna Engberg-Pedersen, and Peter Saville. Berlin: Studio Olafur Eliasson, 2012.

Madison, Deborah. *The Savory Way.* New York: Bantam, 1990.

Madison, Deborah. *Vegetarian Cooking for Everyone.* New York: Broadway, 1997.

Maturana, Humberto R., and Francisco J. Varela. *The Tree of Knowledge: The Biological Roots of Human Understanding.* Boston: Shambhala, 1987.

More than Honey. Dir. Markus Imhoof. Baseline, 2010. Film.

Morton, Oliver. *Eating the Sun: The Everyday Miracle of How Plants Power the Planet.* London: Fourth Estate, 2007.

Pollan, Michael. *Cooked: A Natural History of Transformation.* New York: Penguin Press, 2013.

Pollan, Michael. *In Defense of Food: An Eater's Manifesto.* London: Penguin, 2008.

Pollan, Michael. *The Omnivore's Dilemma: A Natural History of Four Meals.* London: Penguin, 2006.

Raising Compassion. Studio Olafur Eliasson, 2013. Film.

Redzepi, René. *Noma: Time and Place in Nordic Cuisine.* New York: Phaidon, 2010.

The Rodale Book of Composting: Easy Methods for Every Gardener. Ed. Grace Gershuny and Deborah L. Martin. Emmaus, Pennsylvania: Rodale Press, 1992.

Shiva, Vandana. *Soil Not Oil: Environmental Justice in a Time of Climate Crisis.* Cambridge, Massachusetts: South End, 2008.

Shiva, Vandana. "The Future of Food and Seed. 24 April 2011." Web. 5 Nov. 2013.

Shiva, Vandana. *Water Wars: Privatization, Pollution, and Profit.* Cambridge, Massachusetts: South End, 2002.

Singleton Hachisu, Nancy, et al. *Preserving The Japanese Way: Tradition of Salting, Fermenting, and Pickling for the Modern Kitchen.* Kansas City, Missouri: Andrews McMeel Publishing, 2015.

Sonna, Birgit. "In *Vogue Germany,* Olafur Eliasson and Tania Singer Continue Their Discussion of Compassion." *Vogue* (July 2013). www.olafureliasson.net.

Spaull, Susan, and Fiona Burrell. *Leiths Baking Bible.* London: Bloomsbury, 2006.

Studio Olafur Eliasson: An Encyclopedia. Ed. Olafur Eliasson and Anna Engberg-Pedersen. Cologne: Taschen, 2008.

Thun, Maria. *Gardening for Life: The Biodynamic Way.* Trans. Matthew Barton. Gloucestershire, UK: Hawthorn, 1999.

Wagenhofer, Erwin, and Max Annas. *We Feed the World: Was uns das Essen wirklich kostet; Das Buch zum gleichnamigen Film.* Freiburg: Orange-Press, 2006.

Waters, Alice, and David Liittschwager. *Edible Schoolyard: A Universal Idea.* San Francisco: Chronicle, 2008.

Wolfe, Jeremy M., Keith R. Kluender, and Dennis M. Levi. *Sensation and Perception.* Sunderland, Massachusetts: Sinauer Associates, 2011.

Apfeltraum. An organic fruit and vegetable delivery group serving the greater Berlin area. www.abokiste-apfeltraum.de

BioInsel. A green and organic grocery serving the greater Berlin area. www.bio-insel.de

Bio-Saatgut. Ecologically friendly, nongenetically modified seeds. www.bio-saatgut.de

Demeter. A biodynamic food distribution company located in Darmstadt, Germany. www.demeter.net

Greenpeace, campaign against genetic engineering. www.greenpeace.org/international/en/campaigns/agriculture/problem/genetic-engineering/

Institut für Raumexperimente. An experimental art instructional space led by Olafur Eliasson in cooperation with the Berlin University of the Arts. www.raumexperimente.net

Kushi Institute. Center for natural healing and macrobiotic education. www.kushiinstitute.org

Navdanya. Food and seed blog kept by Vandana Shiva. www.navdanya.org

Seed Savers. A nonprofit organization devoted to saving and sharing heirloom seeds. www.seedsavers.net

Soil Association. Charitable organization dedicated to organic food and farming. www.soilassociation.org

Verein zur Erhaltung der Nutzpflanzenvielfalt e.V. Organization for the ecological preservation of agricultural crops. www.nutzpflanzenvielfalt.de

Nico Dockx (BE), artist. Dockx's practice revolves around perception, memory, and translation, concentrating on the thinking and doing of archives. His works – exploring a diversity of media – are often the outcome of collaboration with other artists and friends. He co-curated the Sticky Rice workshop in 2011 and is co-founder of interdisciplinary projects such as Building Transmissions (2001–13), Interfaculty (2007), Extra Academy (2010), A Dog Republic (2011), and La Galerie Imaginaire (2015). He is editing a series of books at the Royal Academy of Fine Arts Antwerp based on his PhD research on the archives of Louwrien Wijers and Egon Hanfstingl, co-published by his independent imprint Curious. His latest publication, *Mobile Autonomy: Exercises in Artists' Self-Organization*, was co-edited with sociologist Pascal Gielen.

Anne Duk Hee Jordan (KR), artist and poet. Jordan studied at the Institut für Raumexperimente from 2009 to 2012 and joined the kitchen team at Studio Olafur Eliasson from 2010 to 2011. Her works, which span installation, photography, video, and performance, focus on questions of identity and are both autobiographical and fictional at the same time. Food – especially potatoes and the rituals, symbols, and rules linked to them – plays a central role in her work, which has been exhibited at the Haus der Kulturen der Welt in Berlin and at the Museum für Angewandte Kunst in Frankfurt, among other spaces. www.dukhee.de

Caroline Eggel (CH), art historian, curator, and Head of Exhibitions and Production at Studio Olafur Eliasson, where she has worked since 2000. Eggel also curates the Grey Sheep project space next to the studio, which was initiated to encourage dialogue between artists associated with the studio and the Institut für Raumexperimente and a local audience.

Olafur Eliasson (DK/IS), artist. Eliasson founded Studio Olafur Eliasson in Berlin in 1995. The studio today employs a team of about ninety people, including craftsmen, architects, artists, archivists, cooks, and art historians. Studio members work with Eliasson to experiment, develop, and produce artworks, exhibitions, and creative projects. In 2009, Eliasson founded the Institut für Raumexperimente, also housed in the studio building. This experimental arts education venture, run in cooperation with the Berlin University of the Arts, ended in 2014. Eliasson founded the social business Little Sun in 2012, a global project that produces and distributes the Little Sun solar lamp for use in off-grid communities and spreads awareness about the need to expand access to sustainable energy to all. Eliasson is currently adjunct professor at the Alle School of Fine Arts and Design in Addis Ababa, Ethiopia. www.olafureliasson.net

Eric Ellingsen (US) – Eric Ellingsen's bio is a sphere.

HEAR
EAR
ART
HEART

www.raumexperimente.net/participant/eric-ellingsen and www.speciesofspace.com

Ivana Franke (HR), artist. Drawing from neuroscience, mathematics, and optics, Franke's works, often light installations, create ambiguous visual phenomena and arresting spatial forms that focus on, as well as confuse, the time-space dynamic in which we live. Franke has exhibited at the Venice Biennale, the Museum of Contemporary Art, Zagreb, and MoMA PS1, New York. She participated in Life Is Space 3, has exhibited work at Grey Sheep, and was awarded the 2009–10 residency at the Institut für Raumexperimente. www.ivanafranke.net

Hu Fang (CN), fiction writer and cofounder and artistic director of Vitamin Creative Space, Guangzhou, and The Pavilion, Beijing. His recent fiction books include *The Troubled Laughter* (2012) and *The Garden of Mirrored Flowers* (2010). He is one of the editors of the book *Olafur Eliasson: Never Tired of Looking at Each Other – Only the Mountain and I.* Coproduced by The Pavilion and Studio Olafur Eliasson in 2012, the book played with multiple layers, juxtapositions, and cutouts to create a book as a spatial experience that involves duration, rhythm, and sequencing and reflects the model of a Chinese scholar's garden. www.vitamincreativespace.com/en

Egon Hanfstingl (DE), artist and cook. Hanfstingl has collaborated with Louwrien Wijers since 1986. In 1993 he founded Harmony Foods for Health and Happiness, a social sculpture project based on fresh, local, organic food. In 2003 he began work on Art=Life=Work, a project based on the archive of Louwrien Wijers. With Asako Iwama and Lauren Maurer, he performed food experiments in 2011 as part of the Sticky Rice workshop at the Institut für Raumexperimente. In 2012 he started Beauty Salon Friesland in Ferwert, a research centre for food, art, and content. In 2014 he invented Blissful Peace Soup for the Festival of Future Nows in Berlin. In 2015 he brought this performance to Paris and Amsterdam.

Asako Iwama (JP), artist and cook. A member of the collective "pop-up café" since 1998, Iwama's artistic practice explores the ontology of eating. Referring to the social aspects of eating as a metaphor for our relation to nature, Iwama seeks to transform the perception of nourishment both aesthetically and epistemologically within her practice and work. Iwama's work has been exhibited at the Haus der Kulturen der Welt in Berlin, the Museum of Contemporary Art in Leipzig, and Den Frie in Copenhagen. Together with Lauren Mauer, Iwama led the kitchen team at Studio Olafur Eliasson between 2005 and 2014 and participated in numerous food experiments in collaboration with the Institut für Raumexperimente. www.asakoiwama.net and popup-cafe.org

Jeremias Holliger (CH), artist. Holliger transferred to the Institut für Raumexperimente in 2010. He focuses on performative processes and the narrative of objects. His artworks include performances, such as *Diagonal Lines, a Decision!*, about uttering the act of producing a work of art, and the video *K*, which deals with the interrelationship of plants, animals, and manmade objects. He participated in a group exhibition at Grey Sheep in 2011, as well as the exhibitions *Basel Research Lab* at Ausstellungsraum Kingental in Basel (2010), *Accidental Accomplishment* at the Institut für Raumexperimente (2013), *The Institute Effect* at the Lisbon Architecture Triennale (2013), and *The End at the Beginning* at Ok Corral in Copenhagen (2013).

Lauren Maurer (US), cook. Maurer moved to Berlin in 1998 and opened a restaurant on Teutoburger Platz. In 2005, she joined the studio team, where she has lead the kitchen with Asako Iwama (until 2014), Christine Bopp, Nora Wulff, and Montse Torredà Martí and has participated in numerous food experiments in collaboration with the Institut für Raumexperimente.

Tor Nørretranders (DK), author. Nørretranders has published extensively on science and its role in society, including the books *The User Illusion* (1998), *The Generous Man* (2005), and *Commonities* (with Søren Hermansen, 2013). In December of 2015 Nørretranders and Olafur Eliasson published a book for a general audience: *Light!* A frequent visitor to the studio, Nørretranders was a participant in Life Is Space 1, 2, 3, and 4, as well as the 2011 Compassion Seminar, and has lectured at the Institut für Raumexperimente. He has published two books on food (in Danish) and is a regular contributor of keynote talks on the history of human food at Rene Redzepi's MAD Symposia. www.tor.dk

René Redzepi (DK) is the chef-patron of Noma, a restaurant in Copenhagen that opened in 2003. His latest project is a Noma residency in Australia beginning in early 2016. René is also the founder of MAD, a not-for-profit organization that works to expand knowledge of food, and VILD MAD, an upcoming digital platform and teaching program, a free resource for learning about, tasting, and sustainably exploring wild food. In an effort to shape his way of cooking, René looks to the local landscape and delves into its ingredients and culture, hoping to rediscover its history and to shape our future. www.noma.dk, www.madfood.co and www.vildmad.dk

Pireeni Sundaralingam (LK), poet, playwright, scientist specializing in cognitive development. Educated at Oxford, Sundaralingam has held research positions at Cornell, UCLA, and MIT. She is the editor of *Indivisible: Contemporary South Asian American Poetry* (winner of the California Book Award 2011). Her own poetry has been published in more than thirty journals and anthologies, including Amnesty International's *100 Poems for Human Rights*. Sundaralingam was a resident at the Institut für Raumexperimente in 2011 and participated in Life is Space 3 and 4. www.pireeni.com

Alice Waters (US), chef, food activist, and author. In 1971, in Berkeley, California, Waters opened the restaurant Chez Panisse, now famous for its organic, locally produced, fresh food. She is the initiator of the Edible Schoolyard, an educational project encouraging children to grow their own fruits and vegetables, with more than 2,000 garden classrooms currently active on six continents. Waters cooked the dinner for the occasion of the opening of *Olafur Eliasson: Take your time* in Chicago in 2009 and visited the studio in 2010, where she participated in the Smell Walk hosted by the Institut für Raumexperimente, and has been a frequent visitor ever since. www.chezpanisse.com and www.edibleschoolyard.org

Christina Werner (DE), founding codirector of the Institut für Raumexperimente. She was assistant to the artistic director of Documenta 11 in Kassel in 2002. From 2007 to 2009, she was Curator for Visual Arts at the Cultural Committee of German Industries, and in charge of the artist award and exhibition series "ars viva." Her work at the Institut für Raumexperimente emphasizes a holistic approach and an interest in transdisciplinary knowledge production within art, bringing together the institute's wide-ranging program of experiments, research, artistic practice, workshops, publications, and food-related projects. www.raumexperimente.net/participant/christina-werner

Image Credits

All photos of the studio and the works of Olafur Eliasson were taken and contributed by the following people: Chiara Dazi, Nico Dockx, Olafur Eliasson, Eric Ellingsen, Raphael Fischer-Dieskau, Thilo Frank, María del Pilar García Ayensa, Jürgen Gebhardt, Anna Sofie Hartmann, Asako Iwama, Biljana Joksimović-Große, Kevin Mertens, Felix Meyer, Marie Sjøvold, Alcuin Stevenson, Christian Uchtmann, Christina Werner, and Jens Ziehe.

All hand drawings and sketches taken from the notebooks of Asako Iwama except where noted below. Elevations of the studio building provided by Studio Olafur Eliasson.

pp. 86–91: Sketches by Jules Gaffney
p. 100: Illustration of the human tongue in J. G. Heck, *The Complete Encyclopedia of Illustration,* New York: Park Lane, 1979
p. 101: X-rays of a human stomach and large intestine from the DRK Krankenhaus, Neuwied
pp. 100–1: Stills from *Concert,* 2013, a film by Amelia Paterson and Studio Olafur Eliasson
p. 124: Diagrams of root and branch cuttings from Nehemiah Grew, *The Anatomy of Plants with an Idea of a Philosophical History of Plants and Several Other Lectures Read Before the Royal Society,* New York: Johnson Reprint Company, 1965
p. 125: Illustration by Wilhelm Troll accompanying Johann Wolfgang von Goethe's *The Metamorphosis of Plants* from Troll, *Goethes Morphologische Schriften,* Jena: Eugen Dietrichs, 1932
pp. 166–7: Drawing of broad bean germination by Don Mackean, from http://www.biology-resources.com/plants-seeds.html
p. 209: *Center image*: illustration of beer yeast under a microscope, "Levûre de bière, vue au microscope," in Jouvet Furne, *Les merveilles de l'industrie ou, Description des principales industries modernes, par Louis Figuier,* Paris, 1873–77
p. 211: Microscope image of *Candida albicans,* a bacterium often found in the human digestive tract. GNU Free Documentation License
p. 213: *Top:* Microscope image of Aspergillus mold. Public domain *Bottom:* Illustration of various microorganisms from *The New Student's Reference Work.* Public domain
p. 215: Diagram of *Lubricus agricola,* earthworm. GNU Free Documentation License
pp. 252–3: Bernd Lintermann, ZKM | Karlsruhe, DNA-sequence, first published as 3-D-image in *Molecular Aesthetics,* edited by Peter Weibel and Ljiljana Fruk, MIT Press, 2013
pp. 264–5: Overprinted pages from Jean-Luc Nancy, "Begrenzte und unendliche Demokratie," *Demokratie? Eine Debatte,* Berlin: Suhrkamp, 2012
pp. 284–5: Mineral Interaction Chart, from orthomolecular.webs.com/elements.htm
pp. 288–9: Minerals photographed at the Mineralische Sammlungen, Technische Universität, Berlin
pp. 338–9: First and second circle (from left): Alcuin Stevenson/Studio Olafur Eliasson; third circle: © European Space Imaging; remaining circles: NASA Visible Earth

Careful inquiries have been made to identify copyright holders for all images. If you are the copyright holder and feel an image has been used without permission, please contact Studio Olafur Eliasson.

Acknowledgments

While too many cooks may spoil the broth, a project this vast could never have been completed without the input of many. Olafur Eliasson would especially like to thank Asako Iwama and Lauren Maurer for their dedication to the studio kitchen over the years, for the thought and care they put into preparing each meal, and for the assiduity with which they assembled the research, recipes, and background material that went into this book. Asako also contributed the majority of the beautiful line drawings printed here. Thanks are also due to Kristina Köper for aiding Lauren and Asako in composing the chapter introductions.

Special thanks go to Andreas Koch and Daniel Wiesmann. Their precise, dynamic design concept successfully brings together many disparate ingredients into a coherent, satisfying whole.

While the photographs in this book stem from a number of photographers, María del Pilar García Ayensa took the vast majority of images of the kitchen and studio that appear here, and her ingenuity in finding new ways of photographing food is admirable. Thanks to Dr. Susanne Herting-Agthe, at the Mineralogische Sammlungen at the TU Berlin, for generously allowing María del Pilar to photograph the minerals there.

Many people have helped Asako and Lauren in the kitchen over the years, but a few deserve special mention here: Thórdís Magnea Jónsdóttir and Aykan Safoğlu, as well as Christine Bopp, Montse Torredà Martí, Julian Bethge, Anne Duk Hee Jordan, and Derrick Wang. Others who have helped with special events include Naoko Ogawa, Stefania Facco, Nicholas Fox Ricciardi, Marie Frohling, and Galina Green. Lynn Peemoeller also deserves thanks for collaborating with the kitchen on food experiments at the Institut für Raumexperimente.

Thanks go to everyone else who contributed recipes, texts, and artworks to this book: Thomas Blumtritt-Hanisch, Gerit Bünnig, Nico Dockx, Caroline Eggel, Eric Ellingsen, Ivana Franke, Egon Hanfstingl, Jeremias Holliger, Hu Fang, Sachiko Iwama, Christina Kim, Al Laufeld, Tor Nørretranders, Pireeni Sundaralingam, Yoshito Wantanabe, Alice Waters, Christina Werner, and Zhang Wei.

Thanks are also due to all members of Studio Olafur Eliasson and to Christina Werner, Eric Ellingsen, and the participants in the Institut für Raumexperimente. Some of you appear in this book, but all of you have come together and shared in the kitchen over the years and gained sustenance and inspiration from its succulent meals.

The publishers would also like to thank Joy Sanchez, Cecilia Molinari, and Isobel McLean for their contributions to the book.

Butter should always be unsalted, unless otherwise specified. All herbs are fresh, unless otherwise specified.

Eggs and individual vegetables and fruits, such as onions and apples, are assumed to be medium, unless otherwise specified. All sugar is white caster (superfine) sugar and all brown sugar is cane or demerara unless otherwise specified.

All cream is 36–40% fat heavy whipping cream unless otherwise specified.

All eggs are large.

All milk is full-fat (whole) at 3% fat, homogenized, and pasteurized, unless otherwise specified.

All yeast is fresh, unless otherwise specified.

All salt is fine sea salt, unless otherwise specified.

Breadcrumbs are always dried, unless otherwise specified.

Cooking times are for guidance only, as individual ovens vary. If using a fan (convection) oven, follow the manufacturer's instructions concerning oven temperatures.

Exercise a high level of caution when following recipes involving any potentially hazardous activity, including the use of high temperatures, open flames, slaked lime, and when deep-frying. In particular, when deep-frying, add food carefully to avoid splashing, wear long sleeves, and never leave the pan unattended.

Some recipes include raw or very lightly cooked eggs, meat, or fish, and fermented products. These should be avoided by the elderly, infants, pregnant women, convalescents, and anyone with an impaired immune system.

Exercise caution when making fermented products, ensuring all equipment is spotlessly clean, and seek expert advice if in any doubt.

When no quantity is specified, for example of oils, salts, and herbs used for finishing dishes or for deepfrying, quantities are discretionary and flexible.

All herbs, shoots, flowers and leaves should be picked fresh from a clean source. Exercise caution when foraging for ingredients; any foraged ingredients should only be eaten if an expert has deemed them safe to eat.

Both metric and imperial measures are used in this book. Follow one set of measurements throughout, not a mixture, as they are not interchangeable.

All spoon and cup measurements are level, unless otherwise stated. 1 teaspoon = 5 ml; 1 tablespoon = 15 ml.

Australian standard tablespoons are 20 ml, so Australian readers are advised to use 3 teaspoons in place of 1 tablespoon when measuring small quantities.

JUN 1 3 2016

Phaidon Press Limited
Regent's Wharf
All Saints Street
London N1 9PA

Phaidon Press Inc.
65 Bleecker Street
New York, NY 10012

www.phaidon.com

First published 2013
© 2016 Phaidon Press Limited

ISBN 978 07148 7111 0

A CIP catalog record for this
book is available from the British
Library and the Library of Con-
gress.

Concept
Olafur Eliasson, Asako Iwama,
Andreas Koch, Daniel Wiesmann

Commissioning Editor
Emily Takoudes

Project Editor
Olga Massov

Managing Editors
Geoffrey Garrison, Camilla
Kragelund, Kristina Köper

Editorial Assistance
William Stewart,
Biljana Joksimović-Grosse

Graphic Design
Andreas Koch, Daniel Wiesmann

Production Controller
Alenka Oblak

Printed in China